WATER RESOURCES BOARD

WATER RESOURCES IN ENGLAND AND WALES

VOLUME 2 : APPENDICES

LONDON: HER MAJESTY'S STATIONERY OFFICE

1973

WATER RESOURCES BOARD PUBLICATION No. 23
© Crown copyright 1973
1SBN 0 11 7800139

WATER RESOURCES IN ENGLAND AND WALES

VOLUME 2 : APPENDICES

Appendix		Page
A	Potential Sources: Technical Aspects	1
B	Potential Sources: Non-Technical Aspects	17
C	Potential Pipeline and Tunnel Aqueducts	23
D	Schedule of Demand Districts and Deficiency Centres	37
E	Cost Assumptions	39
F	The Analysis of Water Resource Systems	43
G	Groundwater for River Regulation and for Conjunctive Use with Surface Water	45
H	Artificial Recharge	47
J	The Demand for Water by Industry	49
K	Diagrams	55

Appendix A Potential sources: Technical aspects

A.1   The tables set out some technical details of the sources which have been considered in the study for this report. They should be read in conjunction with the descriptions in Appendix B.

A.2   Most sources could be developed in different ways within a range of sizes from which a choice can be made. The sizes and yields set out in the tables are those adopted in the study. They are intended to indicate the potential of the sources on a generally comparable basis and should not necessarily be regarded as recommendations. The best choice can be made only after detailed study of all factors including the interaction of sources and the ways in which they could be allocated to meet demands.

A.3   The sources considered in the study for our report are grouped, according to type, in six tables as follows:

Table No	Type of Source
A.1	New inland reservoirs
A.2	Existing reservoirs considered for enlargement
A.3	Existing reservoirs redeployed
A.4	Estuary storage
A.5	Groundwater and artificial recharge of aquifers
A.6	Other types of source (conjunctive use, river abstraction without storage, quality improvement of the Trent and desalination).

A.4   Only some of the sources considered in the study are included in the integrated strategies of source development discussed in Chapter 8 of the main report (Table 16, sheet 1). Sources not so included are indicated with an asterisk in the tables to this appendix. Most of them are, however, included in the regionally based strategies discussed in Chapter 8 (Table 16, sheet 2).

Interpretation of tables

A.5   *Yield to supply*—The continuous yield to supply of the source, taking into account the resource system of which it forms a part; for example, a regulated river or a combination of sources. So far as possible, yields assigned take account of the likely order of development of sources within a single river basin: the combined yield from two or more sources within one basin is not necessarily equal to the sum of the individual source yields considered in isolation. Yields are rounded to the nearest 5 thousand cu.m.d.

A.6   *Storage*—For all new reservoirs usable storage is the capacity between top water level and the lowest level to which the reservoir may be drawn down in the course of normal operation. For enlarged reservoirs existing gross storage, additional usable storage and total storage are given. Storages are rounded to the nearest million cubic metres.

A.7   *Top water level*—The level of the overflow spillway crest assumed for the reservoir (TWL). In the case of bunded storage filled by pumping, the maximum level to which water will be stored. Top water levels are rounded to the nearest metre above ordnance datum (AOD).

A.8   *Maximum height of dam*—The height of the dam crest above the lowest point on the valley floor or stream bed, rounded to the nearest metre.

A.9   *Water surface area*—The water surface area at top water level, except that in bunded reservoirs the embankments are also included. In the case of reservoir enlargements the additional water surface area is the difference between that at existing and proposed top water levels. Areas are rounded to the nearest square kilometre, or tenth of a square kilometre in cases where the area is less than ten square kilometres.

A.10   *Total area of development*—Estuarial storage development will cover areas substantially greater than those needed for the storage works themselves. Consequently, approximate total development areas are given in addition to water surface areas at top water level.

A.11   *Method of supply*—A distinction is drawn between regulation, direct supply and conjunctive use as follows:

 (i) Regulation: the flow in a river is regulated by releasing water from the supporting storage when its own flow is insufficient to support abstractions to supply. In the tables only the rivers directly regulated are named.

 (ii) Direct supply: the source concerned provides a continuous and substantially constant supply by aqueduct direct to the deficiency centre which it serves.

 (iii) Conjunctive use: two or more independent sources are combined to provide a continuous supply by co-ordinating their operation. There will be variations with time in the quantities taken from the component sources and one or other of the sources may at times provide the whole supply. Where a river is one of the independent sources, conjunctive use differs from regulation in that the supporting source (or sources) does not augment and benefit that river but provides an independent supply when needed.

A.12   *Capital cost*—The estimated cost, including all ancillary costs and related charges (other than interest during construction), of providing and constructing the source works. This includes works necessary for filling or recharging the source and for delivering source releases to a regulated river. All other aqueducts have been costed separately. Ancillary costs and related charges include road and service diversions, land acquisition, site investigations, legal charges, engineering and supervision. Provision for periodic replacement of works is not included but is taken into account in discounted unit cost figures (see paragraph A.14). Cost assumptions are set out in Appendix E; costs are based on mid-1972 rates as set out in the table to that appendix.

A.13   *Annual power cost*—The average annual cost of power for filling or recharging a source and for making the supply available at abstraction points prior to transmission.

A.14   *Discounted Unit Cost (DUC)*—Capital cost (allowing for spread of expenditure over the construction period), renewal costs in perpetuity and annual power costs in perpetuity, discounted to a base year at 10 per cent per annum, divided by the quantity of water supplied in each year in perpetuity discounted to the base year at the same rate. In the case either of enlargement or of change of use of existing reservoirs resulting in additional yield, DUCs are based on the increment of yield. For further explanation of the derivation and the significance of discounted unit cost see Appendix E.

Table A.1
New Inland Reservoirs Considered in Study

Reservoir	River authority or conservancy	Regional Water Authority No	Location of reservoir and national grid reference	Yield to supply thousand cu.m.d	Usable storage thousand cu.m	Top water level AOD metres	Maximum height of dam metres	Water surface area sq km	Method of filling	Method of supply
KIELDER WATER	Northumbrian	2	Upper reaches of North Tyne NY 70 87	955	186000	185	50	11	Natural	Regulation of Tyne
IRTHING	Cumberland	1	Upper reaches of Irthing NY 64 69	275	69000	221	37	9·7	Natural	Regulation of Tyne
BORROWBECK	Lancashire	1	Borrow Beck, tributary of Lune NY 59 01	390	71000	274	93	2·3	Partly natural but mainly by pumping from Lune	Regulation of Lune in lower reaches
KILLINGTON*	Lancashire	1	Between Lune and Kent SD 59 89	650	134000	206	36	8·4	Pumping from Lune	Regulation of Lune in lower reaches
HELLIFIELD	Lancashire	1	Middle reaches of Ribble SD 83 55	400	83000	136	19	9·9	Natural	Regulation of Ribble and/or regulation of Wharfe
FARNDALE	Yorkshire	4	Dove, tributary of Yorkshire Derwent SE 66 97	240	36000	173	46	2·0	Partly natural and partly by pumping from lower Dove and Hodge Beck	Regulation of Yorkshire Derwent
BRENIG (A)	Dee and Clwyd	10	Brenig, tributary of Alwen and Dee SH 97 54	225	60000	377	51	4·9	Natural	Regulation of Dee
BRENIG (B)*	Dee and Clwyd	10	As above	505	170000	398	72	7·2	Partly natural and partly by pumping from Alwen and Dee	
BRENIG (A) INCREASED TO BRENIG (B)	Dee and Clwyd	10	As above	280						
CARSINGTON	Trent	3	Henmore Brook, tributary of Dove SK 24 50	180	36000	198	34	2·8	Pumping from Dove	Regulation of Dove
BRUND	Trent	3	Manifold, tributary of Dove SK 10 61	140	27000	256	29	2·1	Partly natural and partly gravity diversion from upper Dove	Regulation of Dove
SINFIN MOOR- TRENT VALLEY PUMPED STORAGE	Trent	3	5 km S of Derby SK 36 31	225	39000	52	16	5·0†	Pumping from Derwent	Direct supply
ASTON-TRENT VALLEY PUMPED STORAGE	Trent	3	7 km SE of Derby SK 40 31	225	39000	59	23	3·8†	Pumping from Derwent	Direct supply
GAM*	Severn	3	Gam, tributary of Banwy, Vyrnwy and Severn SH 98 07	580	112000	275	76	5·0	Part natural, part gravity diversion from Wytham and pumping from Banwy	Regulation of Severn
MARTON POOL*	Severn	3	At head of Rea Brook, tributary of Severn SJ 30 03	475	90000	130	31	5·2	Pumping from Severn	Regulation of Severn
LONGDON MARSH	Severn	3	8 km WNW of Tewkesbury SO 83 37	660	125000	29	19	9·8	Pumping from Severn	Regulation of Severn and direct supply
OTMOOR	Thames	6	10 km NE of Oxford SP 57 14	280	139000	76	20	12†	Pumping from Thames and Cherwell	Mainly regulation of Thames Some direct supply
WADDESDON*	Thames	6	10 km W of Aylesbury SP 71 12	305	150000	107	40	8·1	Pumping from Thames	Direct supply and regulation of Thames
WHITCHURCH*	Thames	6	8 km N of Aylesbury SP 82 20	210	102000	122	36	8·9	Pumping from Thames	Direct supply and regulation of Thames

† Includes area occupied by bund.

Capital cost £ million	Annual power cost £ per thousand cu.m.d	Discounted unit cost (DUC) at rates of take-up indicated new pence per cu.m				Remarks	Reservoir
		Instant-aneous	100 thousand cu.m.d per annum	50 thousand cu.m.d per annum	25 thousand cu.m.d per annum		
10·3	0	0·31	0·45	0·64	1·1	Indirectly, the reservoir will regulate by transfers the Wear and Tees in addition to the Tyne. The Yorkshire Ouse system can be similarly augmented by transfers from the Tees to the Swale	KIELDER WATER
3·0	0	0·29	0·32	0·36	0·45	Assumed for yield assessment that this development follows development of Kielder Water, see above. The Irthing catchment is in Cumberland but a short gravity diversion will allow releases to the South Tyne. Additional rivers can be regulated as for Kielder Water	IRTHING
13·1	155	1·0	1·2	1·4	1·8	Assumed for yield assessment that this development follows development of Lancs Conjunctive Use scheme, see Table A.6 of this appendix	BORROWBECK
29·9	385	1·5	1·9	2·4	3·7	Assumed for yield assessment that this development follows development of Lancs Conjunctive Use scheme, see Table A.6 of this appendix	KILLINGTON★
8·3	0	0·56	0·64	0·77	1·0	Costs given are for regulation of the Ribble. Regulation of the Wharfe would entail the additional cost of a Ribble/Wharfe transfer link. Costs include for road and service diversions but not for diversion of the railway, future plans for which are uncertain	HELLIFIELD
7·2	120	0·87	0·93	1·0	1·2	Yield given is additional to that obtainable from Barmby Sluices, see Table A.6 of this appendix	FARNDALE
7·8	0	0·99	1·1	1·2	1·4	Storage given is the largest feasible for filling within a period of 5½ years without recourse to pumping. River regulation control point for yield stated assumed to be at Manley Hall, as at present By shifting regulation control point to Chester, a further yield of 105 thousand cu.m.d may be obtained from the Dee river system, following construction of Brenig (A), without additional cost	BRENIG (A)
21·0	875 for yield in excess of 225 thousand cu.m.d	1·3	1·4	1·5	1·7	Yield and storage relate to fullest practicable development of site Filling period 5½ years	BRENIG (B)★
13·2	875	1·6	1·7	1·9	2·3		BRENIG (A) INCREASED TO BRENIG (B)
5·5	375	0·88	0·92	0·99	1·1	Could also be filled from and regulate the Derwent, at some additional cost	CARSINGTON
4·5	0	0·87	0·89	0·95	1·1	Could also be filled from the Dove, at some additional cost	BRUND
11·2	210	1·5	1·6	1·7	2·1	Could also be filled from the Dove, at some additional cost	SINFIN MOOR–TRENT VALLEY PUMPED STORAGE
11·2	210	1·5	1·6	1·7	2·1	Could also be filled from the Dove, at some additional cost	ASTON-TRENT VALLEY PUMPED STORAGE
17·0	750 for yield in excess of 210 thousand cu.m.d	0·96	1·1	1·3	1·6		GAM★
14·0	240	0·93	1·1	1·3	1·8	Recent site investigations revealed difficulties which might result in substantially increased cost	MARTON POOL★
9·7	95	0·45	0·54	0·68	1·0	The reservoir can support transfers to the Thames	LONGDON MARSH
43·5	175	4·8	5·2	6·0	7·5	Assumed for yield assessment that this development follows development of Thames groundwater, see Table A.5 of this appendix Yield and cost are intended to give comparability with other schemes. They differ from Metropolitan Water Board estimates	OTMOOR
36·6	950	3·9	4·2	4·7	6·0	Assumed for yield assessment that these developments follow development of Thames groundwater, see Table A.5 of this appendix. If both reservoirs were developed, a capital cost saving of some £10 M would result from joint use of the greater part of the aqueduct system connecting the reservoirs and the Thames	WADDESDON★
30·9	1125	4·6	5·0	5·4	6·4		WHITCHURCH★

Table A.1 continued
New Inland Reservoirs Considered in Study

Reservoir	River authority or conservancy	Regional Water Authority No	Location of reservoir and national grid reference	Yield to supply thousand cu.m.d	Usable storage thousand cu.m	Top water level AOD metres	Maximum height of dam metres	Water surface area sq km	Method of filling	Method of supply
COBBINS BROOK*	Lee	6	Cobbins Brook, tributary of Lee TL 42 02	185	90000	73	38	7·0	Pumping from Thames	Direct supply
GREAT BRADLEY*	Essex	5	At head of Stour TL 67 54	215	99000	106	28	11	Pumping from Ely Ouse	By releases to Stour for re-abstraction
ABBOTSLEY*	Great Ouse	5	Abbotsley Brook, tributary of Bedford Ouse TL 20 58	115	50000	36	18	10	Pumping from Bedford Ouse	Direct supply
MANTON*	Welland and Nene	5	Chater, tributary of Welland SK 88 03	135	83000	115	48	6·1	Pumping from Welland and Nene	Direct supply

Capital cost £ million	Annual power cost £ per thousand cu.m.d	Discounted unit cost (DUC) at rates of take-up indicated new pence per cu.m				Remarks	Reservoir
		Instant-aneous	100 thousand cu.m.d per annum	50 thousand cu.m.d per annum	25 thousand cu.m.d per annum		
20·2	1000	3·3	3·4	3·6	4·1	Assumed for yield assessment that this development follows development of Thames groundwater, see Table A.5 of this appendix	COBBINS BROOK*
17·8	1400	2·9	2·9	3·1	3·5	Assumed for yield assessment that this development follows development of Great Ouse groundwater, see Table A.5 of this appendix	GREAT BRADLEY*
12·9	470	3·3	3·4	3·6	3·9		ABBOTSLEY*
16·4	1150	3·9	4·0	4·2	4·8		MANTON*

Table A.2
Existing Reservoirs Considered for Enlargement in Study

Reservoir	Nature of change in deployment	River authority	Regional Water Authority No	National grid reference of reservoir	Additional yield to supply thousand cu.m.d	Storage thousand cubic metres			Top water level			Maximum height of new dam metres	Additional water surface area sq km
						Existing	Additional	Total	Existing metres AOD	Proposed metres AOD	Increase metres		
HAWESWATER (A)	Part change from direct supply to regulation	Cumberland	1	NY 50 16	395	85000	81000	166000	241	259	18	50	0·9
HAWESWATER (B)					820	85000	169000	254000	241	276	35	67	1·6
HAWESWATER (A) ENLARGED TO HAWESWATER (B)					425		88000	254000		276	17	67	0·7
STOCKS	Direct supply to conjunctive use	Lancashire	1	SD 71 54	See Lancs Conjunctive Use scheme, Table A.6	14000	11000	25000	182	189	7	41	0·5
GRIMWITH	Compensation releases to regulation	Yorkshire	4	SE 06 64	100	3000	17000	20000	269	289	20	45	1·5
CELYN	No change	Dee and Clwyd	10	SH 87 40	260	81000	64000	145000	297	314	17	62	1·2
VYRNWY (A)	Added storage supports regulation	Severn	3	SJ 01 19	570	55000	128000	183000	258	275	17	46	1·9
VYRNWY (B)	Total increased storage supports regulation. Direct supply discontinued	Severn	3	SJ 01 19	730	55000	128000	183000	258	275	17	46	1·9
CLYWEDOG*	No change	Severn	3	SN 91 87	240	50000	50000	100000	283	297	14	81	2·5
NANT-Y-MOCH*	Power generation to joint use for power and regulation	South West Wales	10	SN 75 86	450	23000	73000	96000	340	352	12	67	1·8
CRAIG GOCH	Added storage supports regulation	Wye	10	SN 89 68	1200	9000	231000	240000	317	373	56	95	6·2
TALYBONT*	Total increased storage supports regulation. Direct supply discontinued	Usk	10	SO 10 20	455	12000	91000	103000	189	229	40	70	1·5
BRIANNE	Regulation extended to additional river basin	South West Wales	10	SN 79 48	400	61000	54000	115000	276	294	18	106	3·6

Method of filling additional storage	Method of supply for additional yield	Capital cost £ million	Annual power cost £ per thousand cu.m.d	Discounted unit cost (DUC) at rate of take-up indicated new pence per cu.m				Remarks	Reservoir
				Instant-aneous	100 thousand cu.m.d per annum	50 thousand cu.m.d per annum	25 thousand cu.m.d per annum		
Pumping from Eden or Lune	Regulation of Lune and abstraction in lower reaches	20·5	620	1·8	2·0	2·4	3·1	Direct supply to Manchester from existing storage continued. Assumed that this development follows Lancs Conjunctive Use scheme, see Table A.6 of this appendix. Alternative schemes have been considered with filling either from Eden or Lune, with a range of assumed abstraction conditions and levels of raising. Scheme given here involves filling from Eden with prescribed flow of 1300 thousand cu.m.d and no limit on abstractions of flows in excess of this quantity	HAWESWATER (A)
		28·9	620	1·2	1·5	1·9	2·8		HAWESWATER (B)
		8·4	620	0·76	0·85	0·99	1·3		HAWESWATER (A) ENLARGED TO HAWESWATER (B)
Natural	Conjunctive use with abstractions from Lune, Ribble and ground-water abstractions	2·1	None	—	—	—	—	This scheme is an element of the Lancs Conjunctive Use scheme, see Table A.6 of this appendix	STOCKS
Natural	Regulation of Wharfe	3·5	—	—	—	—	—	Powers are being sought for enlargement of the existing compensation water reservoir and progressive change of use to river regulation. Completion expected by 1976	GRIMWITH
Gravity diversions from Conwy and Lliw	Regulation of Dee	8·5	None	0·94	1·0	1·1	1·4		CELYN
Gravity diversion from Twrch and pumping from Tanat	Regulation of Severn	9·1	320 for yield in excess of 355 thousand cu.m.d	0·49	0·55	0·65	0·87	Existing direct supply of 210 thousand cu.m.d to Liverpool retained. See also Table A.3 of this appendix for Vyrnwy variants not involving enlargement	VYRNWY (A)
Gravity diversions from Twrch and pumping from Tanat	Regulation of Severn	9·1 (but see under Remarks)	320 for yield in excess of 515 thousand cu.m.d	0·38	0·44	0·54	0·78	Existing reservoir yields 210 thousand cu.m.d direct supply to Liverpool. This would be discontinued and replaced by an alternative source. The cost of this is taken into account in development programmes. See also Table A.3 of this appendix for Vyrnwy variants not involving enlargement	VYRNWY (B)
Gravity diversions from Trannon and upper Severn	Regulation of Severn	7·0	None	0·80	0·92	1·1	1·5		CLYWEDOG *
Natural, supplemented by gravity diversions from Gwynedd RA area	Regulation of Severn via gravity tunnel	9·3	None	0·57	0·68	0·81	1·1	Existing CEGB reservoir. Some loss of generating capacity would result from part change of use. Allowance for this has been made in costing	NANT-Y-MOCH *
Natural, gravity diversion from Ystwyth and pumping from Wye and Dulas	Regulation of Severn and Wye	15·7	350 for yield in excess of 410 thousand cu.m.d	0·43	0·59	0·79	1·3	Existing direct supply to Birmingham from Elan group of reservoirs (which includes Craig Goch) maintained	CRAIG GOCH
Natural, and pumping from Usk	Regulation of Usk	14·8	420 for yield in excess of 100 thousand cu.m.d	1·0	1·1	1·4	2·0	Existing reservoir provides 60 thousand cu.m.d direct supply to Gwent Water Board. Cost figures allow for replacement of this supply	TALYBONT *
Natural	Regulation of Wye via gravity tunnel in addition to regulation of Tywi	4·4	None	0·27	0·31	0·37	0·51	The existing dam can be incorporated in the proposed new one	BRIANNE

Table A.3
Existing Reservoirs Deployed

Reservoir	Proposed change of deployment	River authority	Regional Water Authority No	National grid reference of reservoir	Additional yield to supply thousand cu.m.d	Method of providing additional yield	Capital cost on source works for redeployment £ million	Annual power cost £ per thousand cu.m.d	Discounted unit cost (DUC) at rates of take-up indicated new pence per cu.m				Remarks
									Instantaneous	100 thousand cu.m.d per annum	50 thousand cu.m.d per annum	25 thousand cu.m.d per annum	
THIRLMERE	Part change from direct supply to river regulation	Cumberland	1	NY 31 18	180	Regulation of Cumberland Derwent	2·7	None	0·47	0·47	0·49	0·53	Yield, by part change of use to regulation, is obtained at the expense of a small loss of direct supply to Manchester. This loss of yield is provided from an alternative source in development programmes
RIVINGTON GROUP	Augmentation of inflow by pumping from Ribble	Lancashire	1	SD 62 15	180	Direct supply or conjunctive use with other Lancs sources	6·3	1600	1·4	1·4	1·5	1·7	Figures relate to one of several ways in which the yield ascribed could be obtained from the group of reservoirs as part of development of the Lancs Conjunctive Use scheme, see Table A.6 of this appendix
GOUTHWAITE	Change of operating rules to allow regulation	Yorkshire	4	SE 14 68	70	Regulation of Yorkshire Ouse	None	None	—	—	—	—	Bradford CBC compensation reservoir. Agreed change in operating rules for river regulation provides 45 thousand cu.m.d. Associated groundwater development provides further 25 thousand cu.m.d
LADYBOWER	Change of compensation water rules to allow regulation	Trent	3	SK 19 85	50	Regulation of Derbyshire Derwent	None	None	—	—	—	—	Seasonal variation of existing uniform compensation water discharge to give greater summer releases (with consequent winter reduction) can provide a degree of regulation of the Derwent for abstraction in the lower reaches
VYRNWY (C)	Change of compensation water rules to allow regulation	Severn	3	SJ 01 19	25	Regulation of Severn	None	None	—	—	—	—	See also Table A.2 of this appendix for Vyrnwy variants involving enlargement
VYRNWY (D)	Change of use from direct supply to regulation	Severn	3	SJ 01 19	110	Regulation of Severn	See under Remarks	None	—	—	—	—	Existing reservoir yields 210 thousand cu.m.d direct supply to Liverpool. This would be discontinued and replaced by an alternative source. The cost of this is taken into account in development programmes. See also Table A.2 of this appendix for Vyrnwy variants involving enlargement
ELAN VALLEY GROUP	Change of compensation water rules to allow regulation	Wye	10	SN 92 65	120	Regulation of Wye	None	None	—	—	—	—	Seasonal variation of existing uniform compensation water discharge to give greater summer releases (with consequent winter reduction) can provide a degree of regulation of the Wye for downstream abstraction
USK	Change of use from direct supply to regulation and conjunctive use	Usk	10	SN 83 28	100	Regulation of Usk and conjunctive use with abstractions from Tywi	None	See under Remarks	—	—	—	—	Regulation of Usk has prior right to use of stored water. West Glamorgan Water Board served by direct supply when water available, in conjunction with supply from Tywi at other times. Average annual power cost for supply from Tywi estimated as £27000
GRAFHAM WATER	Redeployment of supply for optimal allocation	Great Ouse	5	TL 17 67	285 ‡	Direct supply	—	—	—	—	—	—	Relaxation of statutory allocation rules would allow more effective use to be made of reservoir yield. Yield allows for the construction of a second intake and the growth of effluent to 1981. Additional yield of 185 thousand cu.m.d by 2001 will be generated by growth of effluents
EMPINGHAM	Redeployment of supply for optimal allocation	Welland and Nene	5	SK 94 07	230 ‡	Direct supply (For regulation of Welland and for conjunctive use with Lincs Limestone groundwater, see Table A.6)	—	—	—	—	—	—	Reservoir under construction and should be in operation by 1976. No allowance made for growth of yield due to future increased effluent discharges to Nene
ELY-OUSE TO ESSEX SCHEME (ABBERTON AND HANNINGFIELD)	Redeployment for optimal allocation of supply derived from Ely-Ouse–Essex transfers and storage in reservoirs named	Essex	5	TL 99 19 and TQ 74 99	110 ‡	Direct supply	—	—	—	—	—	—	Ely-Ouse to Essex transmission link completed

‡ Yield of works as at present authorised included for allocation

Table A.4
Estuary Storage Considered in Study

Estuary	Salient features and staging	River authority	Regional Water Authority No	Yield to supply thousand cu.m.d	Usable storage thousand cu.m	Top water level AOD metres	Level of top of embankments AOD metres	Approximate surface area of storage at TWL sq km	Approximate total area of development sq km	Method of filling
MORECAMBE BAY SCHEME IIB	Twin barrages with Warton reservoir	Lancashire	1							
	Whole scheme			2050	273000	As below	As below	59	82	As below
	Stage 1. Leven barrage			540	48000	5·5	7·6	19	21	Natural, from Leven catchment
	Stage 2. Kent barrage			540	56000	5·5	7·6	26	31	Natural, from Kent catchment
	Stage 3. Warton reservoir			970	169000	15·0	16·8	14	30	Pumping, from Leven and Kent
MORECAMBE BAY SCHEME III	River barriers with Cartmel and Warton reservoirs	Lancashire	1							
	Whole scheme			2050	323000	As below	As below	59	75	As below
	Stage 1. Kent barrier and Warton reservoir			950	146000	Kent barrier 5·5 Warton reservoir 15·0	Kent barrier 7·6 Warton reservoir 16·8	28	44	Pumping from Kent to Warton reservoir
	Stage 2. Leven barrier			450	13000	5·5	7·6	6	6	Pumping from Leven to Warton reservoir
	Stage 3. Cartmel reservoir			650	164000	10·5	12·2	25	25	Pumping from Leven
MORECAMBE BAY HYBRID SCHEME	Leven barrage, Kent barrier and Warton reservoir	Lancashire	1							
	Whole scheme			1800	194000	As below	As below	47	65	As below
	Stage 1. Leven barrage			540	48000	5·5	7·6	19	21	Natural, from Leven catchment
	Stage 2. Kent barrier and Warton reservoir			950	146000	Kent barrier 5·5 Warton reservoir 15·0	Kent barrier 7·6 Warton reservoir 16·8	28	44	Pumping from Kent to Warton reservoir
	Stage 3. Leven transfer works			310	—	—	—	—	—	Pumping from Leven barrage to Warton reservoir
DEE ESTUARY	Contracted estuary shape with reservoirs at head of estuary	Dee and Clwyd	10							
	Whole scheme			1080	210000	As below	As below	31	42	Pumping from Dee at tidal barrier for all stages
	Stage 1. High level reservoir at head of estuary			360	44000	17	19	3	}12	
	Stage 2. High level reservoir at head of estuary			220	42000	17	19	4		
	Stage 3. Parkgate low level reservoir			300	74000	10	12	15	19	
	Stage 4. Flint low level reservoir			200	50000	10	12	9	11	

Method of supply	Capital cost £ million	Annual power cost £ per thousand cu.m.d	Discounted unit cost (DUC) at rates of take-up indicated new pence per cu.m				Remarks	Estuary
			Instant-aneous	100 thousand cu.m.d per annum	50 thousand cu.m.d per annum	25 thousand cu.m.d per annum		
								MORECAMBE BAY SCHEME IIB
	75·0		1·1	1·5	1·9	2·8		
	22·4		1·3	1·5	1·9	2·8		
Direct supply but see Remarks	21·6	} 150	1·2	1·5	1·8	2·7		
	31·0		1·0	1·5	2·1	3·6		
							Corresponding with possible choices outlined by the Board in their Report "Morecambe Bay—Estuary Storage", three schemes are here shown. Their distinctive characteristics are as follows:	MORECAMBE BAY SCHEME III
	83·6		1·3	1·9	2·8	5·0	Scheme IIB allows a road crossing but would cause siltation at Heysham	
	43·5		1·5	2·1	3·0	5·0	Scheme III is best on water conservation and general amenity grounds, but offers no opportunity for a road crossing	
Direct supply but see Remarks		} 240					The Hybrid Scheme combines Stage I of Scheme IIB with Stage I of Scheme III. Either of these could be built as a first stage, leaving open the option to proceed later towards completion of the Hybrid Scheme on the one hand, or, on the other, towards Scheme IIB or Scheme III according to the choice already exercised for the first stage	
	18·9		1·2	1·5	1·8	2·4	Costs relate to water conservation works only; they do not include dredging costs which would be associated with Scheme IIB nor highway costs associated with dual purpose schemes	
	21·2		1·0	1·3	1·7	2·6		
							Direct supply has been assumed for costings and yield assessments. Part of the supply may be by river regulation but the effect on source costs and yields would be small	MORECAMBE BAY HYBRID SCHEME
	68·3		1·2	1·7	2·2	3·1		
	22·4		1·3	1·6	1·9	2·8		
Direct supply but see remarks	41·0	} 150	1·4	2·0	2·8	4·7		
	4·9		0·50	0·54	0·62	0·78		
							This scheme is representative of the more likely possibilities for this development. It is not necessarily the one which would be selected	DEE ESTUARY
Direct supply but see Remarks	49·0	170	1·4	1·5	1·7	2·3	Costs relate to water conservation works only and are exclusive of additional costs which would be required for a scheme incorporating a highway. Nor is allowance made for economies consequent on cost sharing for a dual purpose scheme	
	16·7	200	1·5	1·6	1·9	2·5		
	5·6	200	0·81	0·85	0·94	1·1	Direct supply has been assumed for costings and yield assessments. Part of the supply may be by river regulation but the effect on source costs and yields would be small	
	13·0	130	1·3	1·5	1·7	2·1		
	13·7	130	2·1	2·2	2·4	2·8		

Table A.4 continued
Estuary Storage Considered in Study

Estuary	Salient features and staging	River authority	Regional Water Authority No	Yield to supply thousand cu.m.d	Usable storage thousand cu.m	Top water level AOD metres	Level of top of embankments AOD metres	Approximate surface area of storage at TWL sq km	Approximate total area of development sq km	Method of filling
WASH	Bunded reservoirs	Welland and Nene and Great Ouse	5							
	Three stages			1640	495000			55	77	As below
	Stage 1			455	65000			7	10	Pumping from Great Ouse
	Stage 2			545	180000	11·5	14	20	28	Additional pumping from Nene
	Stage 3			640	250000			28	39	Additional pumping from Welland
SOLWAY FIRTH *	Estuary barrage	Cumberland (and Scotland)	1 (and Scotland)	900	90000	4·6	10·7	40	50	Natural
SEVERN ESTUARY * (WELSH GROUNDS)	Bunded reservoirs	Usk and Wye	10	340	59000	10	12	7	10	Pumping from Wye near Chepstow

Method of supply	Capital cost £ million	Annual power cost £ per thousand cu.m.d	Discounted unit cost (DUC) at rates of take-up indicated new pence per cu.m				Remarks	Estuary
			Instant- aneous	100 thousand cu.m.d per annum	50 thousand cu.m.d per annum	25 thousand cu.m.d per annum		
							This scheme is representative of possibilities likely to be favoured following completion of the feasibility study now in progress	WASH
Direct supply	135·2	} >620	2·7	3·2	3·8	4·9	Yields are derived from Consultants' Desk Study Report	
	32·5		2·3	2·7	3·2	4·4	Stage I includes a seawater recirculation scheme which might be constructed as a preliminary stage, yielding about 200 thousand cu.m.d at a capital cost of £9·0 M	
	52·0		3·1	3·8	4·7	6·9	Costs are for water delivered to Denver. They are based on Desk Study estimates updated to 1972. Additionally, however, 15 per cent has been added to the estimated cost of storage works in anticipation of some real cost increase in estimate at Feasibility Study stage	
	50·7		2·6	3·3	4·3	6·5		
Direct supply but see Remarks	11·0	100	0·4	0·5	0·7	1·2	Location and minimum height of barrage are dictated respectively by estuary configuration and tidal levels. Without encroachment on existing tidal marshes, the volume of storage created by a minimum barrage is far in excess of requirements for yield here shown; it would be sufficient in fact for a yield of 1700 thousand cu.m.d. Consequentially, additional yield, if required, could be obtained at minimal cost. Costs are based on a 1966 desk study, updated to 1972 and increased by 30 per cent	SOLWAY FIRTH*
Support of abstractions from Wye at tidal limit	22·0	400	2·0	2·2	·2·5	3·2	This scheme is representative of bunded storage reservoirs in the Severn estuary which could be filled from tidal barriers on the Wye and Usk	SEVERN ESTUARY* (WELSH GROUNDS)

Table A.5
Groundwater Sources and Artificial Recharge of Aquifers Considered in Study

Source	River authority or conservancy	Regional Water Authority No	Location	Aquifer	Yield to supply thousand cu.m.d	Assumed possible annual rate of development thousand cu.m.d	Method of supply	Capital cost £ million	Annual power cost £ per thousand cu.m.d	Discounted unit cost (DUC) new pence per cu.m	Remarks
VALE OF YORK	Yorkshire	4	Vale of York upstream from York	Triassic sandstones	135	25	Regulation of Yorkshire Ouse	2·1	130	0·44	Yield provisionally estimated pending results from pilot scheme at present in progress
SHROPSHIRE	Severn	3	Shropshire	Permo-Triassic sandstones	225	30	Regulation of Severn	5·0	220	0·64	Yield provisionally estimated pending results from pilot scheme at present in progress
FYLDE	Lancashire	1	Fylde Plain	Permo-Triassic sandstones	See under Remarks		Conjunctive use with abstractions from Lune and Ribble and Stocks reservoir	1·4	See under Remarks		This development is an element of the Lancs Conjunctive Use scheme. See Table A.6 for particulars including remarks regarding costs. The long term natural recharge rate of the aquifer is 45 thousand cu.m.d but aquifer storage of about 9500 thousand cu.m can be manipulated to provide by operation of the new wells, up to 90 thousand cu.m.d over limited periods when the flow of the Lune is too low to permit river abstractions
GREAT OUSE CHALK	Great Ouse	5	Ely Ouse catchment	Chalk	330	20	Regulation of Ely Ouse and some direct supply	18·5	320	1·6	Yield based on consideration of pilot scheme results. Assumed that a residual flow of 115 thousand cu.m.d is maintained at Denver all the year round, this residual being acceptable after improvement of industrial effluents at King's Lynn. The cost of this improvement is included in the costs here given
THAMES CHALK AND OOLITE	Thames	6	Upper half of Thames catchment	Chalk and Jurassic limestones	455	80	Regulation of Thames	19·1	90	1·1	Yield based on consideration of pilot scheme results and on assumption that this is next major development in Thames basin
LONDON BASIN RECHARGE	Lee	6	Lower Lee Valley	Chalk and Lower London Tertiary sands	250	25	Conjunctive use with lower Thames water	12·5	810	1·5	Aquifer will be recharged by pumping from Thames. Water recovered from aquifer will be used conjunctively with existing Metropolitan Water Board reservoirs to meet demands in vicinity of recharge area. Costs are for water at recharge area. They include transfer costs for Thames water both for recharge and for conjunctive use element; also additional cost for pre-treatment of recharge water. Yield figures assume this development follows development of Thames groundwater, see above, to 455 thousand cu.m.d. General large scale feasibility and yield to be verified by pilot scheme at present in progress

Table A.6
Other Types of Sources Considered in Study

Development	River Authority	Regional Water Authority No	Nature of proposed development	Stages or elements of development	Yield to supply thousand cu.m.d	Capital cost £ million	Annual power cost £ per thousand cu.m.d	Discounted unit cost (DUC) new pence per cu.m	Remarks
LANCASHIRE CONJUNCTIVE USE	Lancashire	1	Abstractions from Lune near Lancaster, from Permo-Triassic sandstone in Fylde Plain and from Ribble near Mitton all used conjunctively with Stocks reservoir on Hodder, enlarged, and Rivington reservoirs, redeployed	Stage 1 Development of Lune and Permo-Triassic sandstone abstractions, raising of Stocks reservoir and construction of Lune/Wyre transmission link	150		See under Remarks		The Lancs Conjunctive Use scheme consists of a complex of existing and new sources, transmission links, treatment works, etc., costed under the respective headings in the source development programmes. See Table A.2 for enlargement of Stocks reservoir, Table A.3 for redeployment of the Rivington group of reservoirs, and Table A.5 for Fylde Plain groundwater development
				Stage 2 Further development of Stage 1 sources, abstractions from Ribble and extension of transmission system	120		See under Remarks		
				Stage 3 Augmentation, from Ribble, of inflow to Rivington reservoirs and redeployment of reservoirs	180 See Table A.3 of this appendix		See under Remarks		
WELLAND CONJUNCTIVE USE (Empingham and Lincs Limestone)	Welland and Nene	5	Conjunctive use of abstractions from Empingham, Lincolnshire Limestone and Welland		90		See under Remarks		Scheme involves conjunctive use of surface storage at Empingham reservoir, see Table A.3 with intermittent abstractions from Lincs Limestone in support of abstractions from the Welland, costed under the respective headings in the source development programmes. The scheme will mean changing some existing continuous groundwater abstractions to surface abstractions supported by groundwater as the aquifer is fully developed by existing licensed abstractions
BARMBY SLUICES	Yorkshire	4	Abstractions, up to total flow in low flow periods, from Derwent at Barmby sluices, near outfall to Yorkshire Ouse		145	0·8	Nominal	0·2	
MIDDLE TRENT CONJUNCTIVE USE*	Trent	3	Abstractions from Derwent used conjunctively with abstractions from Triassic sandstones		180	11·2	1600	2·4	Yield shown is increase over present yield of 180 thousand cu.m.d obtained by abstraction from Triassic sandstones. Costs are for water at Nottingham, they include for treatment works which, on account of the nature of the scheme, are additional to those normally required in orthodox surface abstraction schemes
RIVER TRENT (DIRECT ABSTRACTIONS)	Trent	3	Advanced treatment of water abstracted directly from the Trent, at riverside location as required		1100	9·3	1465	0·64	The suitability of the Trent as a source for potable supply remains to be established. Treatment plant would be provided in units of about 125 thousand cu.m.d and the DUC is based on an assumed rate of take-up of about 50 thousand cu.m.d per annum
RIVER TRENT (BUNTER SANDSTONE RECHARGE)	Trent	3	Purification of Trent water by pre-treatment followed by percolation through and temporary storage in Triassic sandstones	Recharge area 5 km NE of Worksop, SK 62 81	545	18·5	3400	2·0	Although suitability of Trent water for potable supply remains to be established, quality would be improved and the resulting water may be more acceptable for potable supplies if the water is artificially charged into the Triassic sandstones with pre-liminary biological and some final chemical treatment. The area required for infiltration basins is about 6 sq km
				Recharge area between Nottingham and Mansfield, SK 58 53	135	4·6	3800	2·0	
DESALINATION OF SEA WATER	Great Ouse and Essex	5	Provision as required of coastal desalination plants, probably distillation plants, of about 25 thousand cu.m.d capacity each	Sites at southern corner of Wash and sites on Blackwater estuary	1155 used in development programme	179	17000	10	Costs are based on recent estimates for VCE (vapour compression evaporation), a process which is not yet commercially established. Production by the commercially established MSF (multi-stage flash distillation) process would lead to costs some 40 per cent higher than here indicated. DUC assumes that yield of each new unit is taken up within one year

Appendix B Potential sources: Non-technical aspects

B.1 This appendix provides further information to supplement the technical and cost data set out in Appendix A. It incorporates views put to us by the Nature Conservancy; the Countryside Commission; the Ministry of Agriculture, Fisheries and Food and the National Farmers' Union; local planning authorities and officers; and local amenity and other interests. We have ourselves visited all the main sites for reservoirs and other major developments and made our own assessments.

B.2 Sources which are referred to in the main report are indicated: in those cases these notes should be read in conjunction with the appropriate paragraphs of the report.

New Reservoirs

Kielder (paragraphs 190/191; 246)[1]
B.3 The site is on the river North Tyne in Kielder Forest in Northumberland. The land is mainly owned by the Forestry Commission (who do not object to the proposal). The area is heavily wooded with conifer and the agricultural land is mainly low grade down to pasture. The proposed reservoir area of about 11 sq km contains about seventy properties, of which about forty five belong to the Forestry Commission for occupation by their employees: the occupants would be re-housed nearby. The remaining properties include some farm buildings and several holiday cottages.

B.4 The Countryside Commission would generally welcome the reservoir as an attractive landscape feature with considerable recreation potential; and because it would be large enough to reduce the need for other reservoirs, some of which might be proposed in national parks. The Nature Conservancy have no objection to the scheme. The Ministry of Agriculture, Fisheries and Food say that the quality of the land and type of holding is such that they are not able to suggest a reservoir site less damaging to agriculture: the National Farmers' Union withdrew their objection at the Public Inquiry. The local planning authority are in favour of the scheme.

Irthing (paragraphs 191; 258)
B.5 This site lies on the upper reaches of the river Irthing in Cumberland. The reservoir area of 10 sq km is in a wild and bleak landscape covered with peat, rough moorland grasses and areas of moss. The dam would have a concrete centre section with earth embankment flanks across a steep gorge.

B.6 The site is used for cattle and sheep grazing. It is of poor quality, classified Grade 5. Two farms and less than a dozen people would be affected. There are no scheduled buildings or ancient monuments in the reservoir area. The Nature Conservancy would accept the proposal reluctantly, because of the unique nature of the vegetation, particularly in the area known as the Wou; they would prefer Kielder. The proposal would have some recreational potential, but less than Kielder.

Borrowbeck (paragraphs 258/259)
B.7 The site comprises a steep sided valley just outside the Lake District National Park, but in an area valued for its landscape. The dam would be large—560 m long and 93 m high—but top water level need not encroach on the National Park or interfere with the A6 trunk road. The water area would be relatively small—some 2·3 sq km. Two farms, one of which is unoccupied, would be severely affected and seven others, together with common grazing land, would suffer some loss. Most of the land is used for rough grazing and is graded 5. The Countryside Commission would prefer this site not to be

developed because of the effect on the landscape. The site has little recreational potential.

Killington
B.8 The site is in Westmorland, outside the Lake District National Park, on the watershed between the catchments of the river Lune and the river Kent. There is already a small reservoir there, which is the main storage supplying the Lancaster canal. The site adjoins the M6. The reservoir would be constructed by clay fill embankments between the natural rock ridges and "drumlins" on the plateau. The long embankments and aqueduct links make this an expensive source in comparison with potential alternatives.

B.9 The area of the reservoir would be 8·4 sq km. The land affected is mainly agricultural, Grades 4 and 5. It contains a site of special scientific interest at Burn Beck Moss, and the Nature Conservancy would be reluctant to accept the proposal unless it removed the threat to Haweswater, Morecambe Bay or Solway. A reservoir here would have considerable recreational potential, although additional works might be required to limit drawdown. Landscaping could be both difficult and expensive.

Hellifield (paragraphs 258/259)
B.10 This site is on the river Ribble downstream of Settle, beside the A65 Leeds–Kendal trunk road, and a branch railway line to Carnforth. A dam at Deep Dale point, only about 170 m long and 19 m high, would form a shallow reservoir of some 10 sq km. Both the railway and roads would have to be moved.

B.11 The site has a very high recreational potential because it is so near to the industrial areas of Lancashire and Yorkshire. It might become a regional recreation centre.

B.12 The reservoir area is used mainly for livestock farming and is classified Grade 3. Six farms are wholly or partially within the affected area and a reservoir here would be strongly opposed by agricultural interests.

Farndale (paragraphs 188; 214)
B.13 The Yorkshire River Authority's Bill to authorise a reservoir at Farndale in the North York Moors National Park was rejected by Parliament in 1970. The valley is highly regarded for its landscape, including the wild daffodils which grow in the lower part of the valley, mainly downstream of the reservoir site. Any new proposal for this site is likely to be opposed by the Countryside Commission and other amenity interests. The agricultural land is Grade 4 and five farms would be affected. The reservoir would cover 2 sq km.

Carsington and Brund (paragraphs 201/202; 262–264)
B.14 These two sites are alternatives for the next source for the north and east Midlands. Brund is in the Peak District National Park; Carsington is just outside it. Both sites are in pleasant open valleys, generally Grade 4 agricultural land used for grazing. Both sites contain some farm buildings and dwellings. The loss to agriculture would be rather higher at Brund and the Ministry of Agriculture, Fisheries and Food would therefore prefer Carsington. The Countryside Commission regard both proposals as objectionable on landscape grounds: they regard Carsington as marginally less objectionable and think that this site offers some recreational potential.

Trent Valley (Aston and Sinfin Moor) (paragraphs 262–265)
B.15 These sites lie about 7 km south east and 5 km south of the centre of Derby respectively, in the triangle formed by the town of

---

1 Paragraph numbers in brackets indicate references in the main report.

Derby and the rivers Trent and Derwent. Sinfin Moor is about 4 km west of Aston and is close to housing development on the southern outskirts of Derby.

B.16   A reservoir at Aston would require an embankment about 5 km long, with a maximum height of 21 m. It would occupy about 4 sq km mainly of agricultural land in Grades 2 and 3. There are two farms and three other properties within the area. The site is crossed by a class B road and an unclassified road; both could be diverted outside the embankment. The intended route of the M42 Nottingham–Birmingham motorway crosses the south east edge of the site; the reservoir embankment on that side could be aligned parallel to and immediately adjacent to the motorway.

B.17   At Sinfin Moor the embankments would be over 7 km long with a maximum height of 16 m. The area of some 5 sq km is mainly agricultural land, Grades 2 and 3, and contains three farms. The site is crossed by two unclassified roads, by several electricity transmission lines and underground services, all of which would have to be diverted.

B.18   Both sites are on land which may be required for the expansion of Derby, but the use of one site for a reservoir should not constitute a major obstacle to urban development. The Ministry of Agriculture, Fisheries and Food would object to development at either site because of the loss to agriculture. There is potential for a limited amount of recreational development, which would be an advantage in an area where there is a scarcity of open water. There would be ready access from both the M1 and proposed M42 motorways, especially to Aston.

B.19   On present evidence, subject to detailed investigation of the site, Aston seems the better choice of the two. It would take less land, it is further from Derby and from both existing and likely future housing developments and it is nearer the river Derwent with a consequently shorter pipeline for filling.

Gam (paragraph 199)
B.20   We recommended investigation of this site in our report on Wales and the Midlands as a possible alternative to the enlargement of Craig Goch. The site considered in this study covers an area of about 5 sq km and contains twelve farms and dwellings and a chapel. The land is used for hill farming and is generally of a low grading: the Ministry of Agriculture, Fisheries and Food would however object to development of this site rather than one of the proposed enlargements. The site is in fine landscape close to the Snowdonia National Park. The Countryside Commission consider, however, that a carefully designed reservoir could fit in satisfactorily without great loss of amenity.

Marton Pool (paragraph 199)
B.21   This site also was recommended similarly for investigation as an alternative to Craig Goch. The reservoir would be formed by building two embankments to seal off an area of flat land between high ground east of the village of Marton, 8 km south east of Welshpool at the head of the Rea Brook, a small tributary of the river Severn. The reservoir would cover an area of just over 5 sq km of medium grade agricultural land, much of which has recently been improved by drainage. Several houses, cottages and farms would be affected.

B.22   There would be agricultural objections to a reservoir here. The Countryside Commission consider that the embankments, which would be visible from the Shropshire Hills Area of Outstanding Natural Beauty, would be visually objectionable; and that recreational potential would be limited. The local planning authority do not share the Commission's view concerning recreation potential, although they see other problems. Site investigations have indicated that foundation conditions are difficult and costs would be high in comparison with several alternatives.

Longdon Marsh (paragraphs 250; 268)
B.23   This site lies in a natural bowl about 8 km north west of Tewkesbury and 4 km west of the river Severn. The reservoir would be formed by closing gaps in the high ground with low banks, with a main embankment 18 m high on the western side. The reservoir would have an area of about 10 sq km.

B.24   The proposal has not aroused objections on amenity grounds, although the Countryside Commission have expressed concern both about the possible effects of drawdown and about the effect on the view from the Malvern Hills Area of Outstanding Natural Beauty. They would wish to comment again when more details of exact location and design are known. The County Planning Officer, on a superficial assessment only, suggests that a reservoir here could provide the one element missing from the landscape in the area—namely a sheet of water—and the view from the Malvern Hills could be enhanced accordingly. Easy access from motorways would add appreciably to the recreational potential of the site. A reservoir here could have potential as a wintering area for wildfowl.

B.25   The land involved is mainly agricultural which is being improved by land drainage generally to Grade 3. The Ministry of Agriculture, Fisheries and Food would regard a reservoir on this site as damaging. The alignment of the embankments can, however, be adjusted to reduce the number of dwellings to be flooded to no more than five or six.

Otmoor (paragraphs 266–269)
B.26   The site is about 10 km north east of Oxford and is a flat, low-lying area, mainly rough grassland and marshland. Until recently it was used as a bombing range and part is still used as a rifle range. Agriculturally the land is generally of low quality in Grade 5, except in those parts which have recently been successfully drained. The Ministry of Agriculture, Fisheries and Food would regard this site as the least damaging of those considered in the South East.

B.27   The scheme considered in this study would involve flooding an area of 12 sq km by means of embankments extending for about 12 km and up to 20 m high. The site contains five farms and is crossed by a few minor roads and a power line. 8 sq km of marshland in the centre of the site is scheduled as a site of special scientific interest. Just outside the southern boundary there is a sixteenth century moated farm known alternatively as Lower Park Farm and as Beckley Grange, which is protected by a Grade 1 preservation order under the Town and Country Planning Acts.

B.28   The possibility of developing a reservoir at Otmoor has aroused strenuous opposition from local amenity and other preservationist interests. The Nature Conservancy would strongly oppose the proposal. The Countryside Commission do not, however, think that there are strong grounds for landscape objection and consider that there is substantial recreational potential. The projected route of the M40 motorway crosses the south western part of the area.

Waddesdon and Whitchurch
B.29   These two sites lie about 12 km apart in the upper part of the river Thame catchment near Aylesbury. They may both be considered as direct alternatives to Otmoor.

B.30   The Waddesdon site lies in the valley of a small tributary of the river Thame. The reservoir would flood about 8 sq km of mainly average quality (Grade 3) land down to pasture. The area contains seven farms and a minor road which would have to be diverted. Waddesdon Manor, a National Trust property, lies outside the area which would be flooded. The Countryside Commission regard this proposal as objectionable on landscape grounds.

B.31   The Whitchurch reservoir would be at the head of the valley of the river Thame and would flood 9 sq km of mainly Grade 4 agricultural land. Seven agricultural holdings would be affected, but no farm buildings lost. The site is crossed by three minor roads and there is a radiotelephone establishment close to it at Creslow Manor. The Countryside Commission would prefer this site to Waddesdon, partly because of its higher recreational potential.

B.32   The effect on agricultural land and buildings of a reservoir at Waddesdon would be considerably greater than at Otmoor; the effect at Whitchurch would be about the same but for a smaller scheme. Both sites are remote from the Thames and would require long aqueducts. We prefer Otmoor to either.

Cobbins Brook
B.33   Cobbins Brook is a small tributary of the river Lee and lies a short distance to the west of Epping. The reservoir would extend over

an area of 7 sq km of Grade 3 agricultural land and would submerge up to eight farms and seventeen other dwellings together with various roads and power lines; a larger reservoir would encroach on Epping Forest.

B.34   This scheme would attract strong agricultural and amenity objections. The Countryside Commission would regard the loss of relatively unspoilt country so close to London as serious and would regard a reservoir here as an incongruous visual intrusion, notwithstanding its very high recreational potential.

B.35   Together with relatively high costs, these considerations rule out this source for inclusion in an integrated national strategy. It is however necessary to include it in programmes providing for self-sufficiency of the Thames Water Authority.

Great Bradley
B.36   This reservoir at the head of the river Stour on the Cambridgeshire/Suffolk border would flood over 11 sq km of good quality (Grade 2) farm land with some woodland. Three large farms would lose most of their land and cease to be viable; another twenty would also be affected. Twenty two dwellings, including much of the village of Carlton, would be flooded. A statutory nature conservation site would also be affected. The Countryside Commission see no objection to the scheme from the point of view of landscape and recreational potential would be high.

B.37   Construction of a reservoir on this site is technically feasible, but would be expensive because of geological conditions. This factor, together with the agricultural and social objections, rule out this site from consideration for a national strategy. It might, however, be needed for a strategy of regional self-sufficiency.

Abbotsley
B.38   The reservoir would lie in the flat valley of the Abbotsley Brook, some 10 km south of Grafham Water but on the east side of the Bedford Ouse. It would involve flooding about 10 sq km of good (Grade 2) arable land and the Ministry of Agriculture, Fisheries and Food would object. Apart from the main earth dam, a subsidiary embankment 1·7 km long and 9 m high would be necessary to avoid flooding the village of Abbotsley. Like Great Bradley it might be necessary, despite its high cost and extensive demands on good farm land, in a strategy of regional self-sufficiency.

Manton
B.39   This reservoir would lie a short distance upstream of the village of Manton in the valley of the river Chater, a tributary of the river Welland. The dam would be about 1 km from the south west end of the new Empingham reservoir. The water area would be about 6 sq km on land which is mainly Grade 3 arable farm land. Nine farm holdings would be totally inundated, and a further eleven affected. The Countryside Commission see no cause for objection on landscape grounds and point to the reservoir's high recreational potential.

B.40   It is, however, relatively expensive, and this together with its high demands on agricultural land and its proximity to Empingham in our view rule it out from consideration. Again, however, it might be necessary in a strategy of self-sufficiency.

Reservoir Enlargements
Haweswater (paragraphs 258–261)
B.41   Manchester Corporation's Haweswater reservoir lies within the Lake District National Park on the headwaters of the river Lowther, a tributary of the river Eden. Consulting engineers have established the feasibility of constructing a new dam immediately downstream of the existing one. The dam could be raised in either one or two stages. The new dam would be large: some 700 m long and 70 m high. The yield of the new reservoir would also be large, comparable with a major stage of estuary storage. The enlarged reservoir would be refilled by pumping from the river Eden or the river Lune: in either case abstraction conditions would need to take account of the possible effects on fisheries.

B.42   The enlarged reservoir would require less than 2 sq km of additional land. The existing hotel, road and footpaths would be sub-

merged, but there would be little effect on agricultural land and other properties. A site of special scientific interest, Naddle Low Forest, would be affected and the Nature Conservancy would on this account object to the enlargement unless it were essential to save Morecambe Bay or Solway.

B.43   The possibility of enlarging Haweswater has already aroused strong opposition. The Countryside Commission would regard raising the dam on the scale envisaged as a further serious intrusion on the landscape of the national park and suggest that the new higher dam and the greater water area would be out of scale with the surrounding hills; they would object to this enlargement.

Stocks
B.44   Raising the level of Stocks reservoir owned by the Fylde Water Board is an essential part of the Lancashire Conjunctive Use Scheme. The reservoir lies in the Forest of Bowland Area of Outstanding Natural Beauty. The increase proposed is relatively small and the Countryside Commission say that an increase of up to about 10 m is unlikely to result in a lake which would be out of scale with the landscape.

Llyn Celyn
B.45   Llyn Celyn is owned by Liverpool Corporation. It lies on the Afon Tryweryn in the Snowdonia National Park and is used to regulate the river Dee. The present capacity could be nearly doubled by raising the dam 17 m. This would require about 1·2 sq km of additional land, which contains a few properties and a Class B road. The Countryside Commission would accept a limited raising of the existing dam; a new dam downstream of the present one would be more difficult to assimilate into the landscape.

B.46   The scheme has not yet been investigated in detail, but it is likely that the reservoir would have to be taken out of service while the work was done. It can therefore only be regarded as a proposition for the longer term.

Vyrnwy (paragraphs 214; 250; 267)
B.47   The capacity of Liverpool Corporation's direct supply reservoir, Lake Vyrnwy, could be more than trebled by raising the top water level by 17 m. This would submerge about 2 sq km of land surrounding the present reservoir. The land is mainly forest but with some hill pasture. Alternatively, without enlargement, the use of the reservoir could be changed from direct supply to regulation of the river Severn, with a consequent net gain to yield of 110 thousand cu.m.d.

B.48   Raising the dam by 17 m would probably be visually acceptable and the Countryside Commission would not object. It would, however, raise formidable social problems including the need to re-site, for the second time, much of the village of Llanwddyn. It would involve rebuilding the road around the reservoir. Moreover, the existing dam, completed in 1891, was the first major masonry dam built in this country and is a much prized example of Victorian civil engineering.

Clywedog (paragraph 250)
B.49   Clywedog reservoir is used to regulate the river Severn. It is in the recently designated[1] Cambrian Mountains National Park. Raising the existing dam by 14 m would double the present storage and would submerge another 2·5 sq km of mostly hill pasture, together with about six farms and dwellings, a chapel and burial ground, and a petrol filling station. The Countryside Commission regard the present reservoir as large and out of scale with its surroundings. An enlargement would accentuate this and the Commission would prefer this reservoir not to be extended.

Nant y Moch (paragraph 199)
B.50   Nant y Moch reservoir is the main storage in the Central Electricity Generating Board's Rheidol hydro-electric scheme. It is in the headwaters of the Afon Rheidol, close to the headwaters of the rivers Wye and Severn on Pumlumon Fawr in the proposed Cambrian Mountains National Park. The enlargement now under investigation would involve an increase in top water level of 12 m. The additional area flooded would be less than 2 sq km. The land is rough hill grazing

---

1 The designation of the Cambrian Mountains National Park has yet to be confirmed by the Secretary of State for Wales.

and contains no dwellings. The Countryside Commission consider, however, that an increase of this order would be visually objectionable and they would therefore oppose it.

B.51   This source is at present ruled out of consideration by doubts about the quality of the water which would be stored in an enlarged reservoir. It is in an area which has in the past been extensively mined for lead and zinc, and this might cause metal contamination. It may be possible in the future to control this problem.

Craig Goch (paragraphs 198/199; 251; 254; 268)
B.52   Craig Goch is the uppermost of the group of direct supply reservoirs owned by Birmingham Corporation in the Elan Valley. It was built in the last century and is small both in relation to its catchment and to the group of reservoirs as a whole. It could be made very much bigger. An increase in top water level of about 56 m would give a total capacity about twenty five times that of the present reservoir. The enlarged water area would be about 6·2 sq km compared with the present 1 sq km. The new reservoir would be twice as long and four times as wide as the present one.

B.53   Craig Goch lies in the proposed Cambrian Mountains National Park. The landscape change would not, however, in the view of the Countryside Commission give rise to serious objection. The land (which is all owned by Birmingham Corporation) is low grade peaty moorland used for sheep grazing. The area which would be flooded contains three farms and ten other holdings would be affected. An ancient track known as the Monk's Road crosses the area.

Talybont
B.54   This direct supply reservoir owned by the Gwent Water Board lies on a tributary of the river Usk in the Brecon Beacons National Park. An increase in top water level of 40 m would require about 1·5 sq km of additional land, mainly hill grazing and woodland. No dwellings would be involved. The Countryside Commission would object to raising the level on this scale. A Nature Conservancy site of special scientific interest would also be affected.

B.55   This site is badly placed to meet any demands other than those in south east Wales, and those can be better and more cheaply met by sources such as Craig Goch and Brianne, which can supply other centres at the same time. It is not therefore included in any of the alternative programmes.

Llyn Brianne (paragraph 248)
B.56   This is a recently completed reservoir in the proposed Cambrian Mountains National Park. It is owned by the West Glamorgan Water Board and used to regulate the river Tywi. In the construction of the dam provision was made for it to be raised, and the consulting engineers consider that raising it by 18 m would be feasible. The increase in level would involve flooding another 3·6 sq km of land, but would involve no buildings. In the view of the Countryside Commission the present reservoir has so damaged the landscape that an enlargement would make no difference.

Estuary Storage
Morecambe Bay (paragraphs 256/257)
B.57   We published our report on the full feasibility study of Morecambe Bay in February 1972. This was a comprehensive study, covering in addition to engineering considerations the wider economic and social implications of the proposed schemes and their potential effects on the ecology and on the environment. The study established the feasibility of developing Morecambe Bay for water storage in a number of ways, using either reservoirs behind barrages or bunded reservoirs on the shores of the bay or a combination of both.

B.58   In our view the choice lay between the three schemes set out in Appendix A:
  (i)   Scheme IIB involves barrages across both the Leven and Kent estuaries and a pumped storage reservoir at Warton. It would provide a road crossing and would be acceptable on water conservation grounds, but the risk of siltation at Heysham would be high;
  (ii) Scheme III has smaller tidal barriers further upstream on both estuaries and pumped storage reservoirs at both Warton and Cartmel. It avoids the risk of siltation at Heysham but precludes the possibility of a road crossing;
  (iii) The hybrid scheme consists of the Leven barrage of Scheme IIB and the Kent barrier of III together with a single reservoir at Warton. A final decision between this hybrid scheme and IIB could be taken at a later date, allowing time to resolve the issue between the benefits of a road crossing and the disadvantages associated with it.

B.59   Any one of these schemes would have serious effects on the amenities of the bay area—although there would also be substantial recreational potential—and on ecology. The bay is of international importance as the habitat and feeding grounds of migratory wading birds. The Nature Conservancy, who contributed to the feasibility study, are opposed to any development in the bay. If it had to be developed, they would prefer a scheme which did not involve the Cartmel Peninsula.

B.60   The study established that the most important non-water benefit was undoubtedly the possibility of improved road access to the Furness peninsula. But any scheme incorporating a road crossing would cause siltation which could jeopardise access by sea to Heysham Harbour.

B.61   The conclusions of our report were as follows:
  (a)   If Morecambe Bay is to be used for freshwater storage, then on water resources grounds and for general environmental reasons we would prefer a development starting with the Kent half of Scheme III (Kent barrier, Warton storage) and leading ultimately to completion of Scheme III (Leven barrier, Cartmel storage, no road crossing) or of the hybrid scheme (Leven barrage, no road crossing).
  (b)   If the benefits of a road crossing are held on grounds of regional economic policy to outweigh the disadvantages associated with it, then the best choice in our view would be Scheme IIB (Kent and Leven barrages, Warton storage, road crossing). If a decision on the Kent half of the scheme could be deferred, development could start with the Leven barrage and lead to the completion of either Scheme IIB (Kent barrage, Warton storage, road crossing) or the hybrid scheme (Kent barrier, Warton storage, no road crossing).

The Dee (paragraphs 253–255; 261)
B.62   In March 1971 consulting engineers appointed jointly by the Department of the Environment, Welsh Office and certain local authorities reported on schemes for developing the estuary. Their report favoured a single road crossing from Flint to Burton together with water storage in embanked reservoirs concentrated towards the head of the estuary. The exact arrangement and location of the water storage would depend upon whether it was necessary to reserve land at the head of the estuary either for extending the Shotton Steel Works or for cooling ponds for a new nuclear power station; either of these possibilities (neither of which now seems likely) would necessitate siting the water storage further down the estuary and would increase the cost of the scheme. Integrated development of road and water supply schemes would achieve economies compared with separate single purpose schemes meeting the same objectives, but this does not affect the choice to be made for water conservation purposes.

B.63   The scheme considered in this report comprises four reservoirs, each constituting a stage of development, located in the upper part of the estuary. Two, sited near Burton at the head of the estuary upstream of the Flint–Burton road crossing line, are relatively deep. The other two are shallower, and are sited downstream of this line on either side of the river channel. All four would be filled by pumping from upstream of a tidal sluice on the line of the road crossing. The reservoirs would be separated from the estuary shore by meres which would reduce the visual impact of the embankments.

B.64   The total area of development would be about 42 sq km. Development on this scale would clearly have a large impact on both the natural and man-made environment over a wide area, extending well beyond the Dee Estuary itself, especially if the water conservation scheme is associated with a road crossing. The report examined the effects of a new road crossing on travelling, industry and housing: it would generate considerable benefits. Moreover, the proposed meres would provide opportunities for recreational development.

B.65   Unlike Morecambe Bay and the Wash the head of the Dee Estuary is already a highly developed industrial area. Its seaward end is an undeveloped area of sand and mud flats, difficult of access, which few people can enjoy. It is of international importance as a habitat and winter feeding ground for wading birds and wildfowl. The Nature Conservancy advise, however, that if development is concentrated at the head of the estuary, interference will be kept to a minimum and any reduction in feeding grounds could partly be offset by conservation areas of wet land habitat in the proposed meres. They emphasise, however, that they have not studied the ecological implications of development in this estuary in the same detail as at Morecambe Bay or the Wash.

The Wash (paragraphs 269; 271)
B.66   The desk study undertaken in 1968–69 established that freshwater could best be stored in the Wash in three or four bunded reservoirs just off-shore between the outfalls of the rivers Great Ouse and Welland. In 1971 the Government authorised us to undertake a full feasibility study and this is now in progress. It involves physical investigation of the engineering feasibility of development in the Wash and investigations of the ecological, economic and social implications of any development.

B.67   Appendix A sets out details of the provisional scheme outlined in the consultants' report on the desk study. The four reservoirs would cover in all an area of approximately 100 sq km, about 15 per cent of the total area of the Wash. The strip of land between the reservoirs and the present sea defence bank could be reclaimed for agriculture or be used for fisheries, for recreation or for nature conservation.

Solway (paragraphs 190; 221)
B.68   In 1966 a desk study indicated the possibility of constructing a barrage across the Solway Firth on the line of the former railway viaduct where the Firth narrows to a width of about 2 km between Seafield in Scotland and Bowness in Cumberland. Such a barrage might incorporate a road crossing to shorten the route between Scotland and the Cumberland coast.

B.69   Development need not involve flooding the areas of grazing or the salt marshes which are of value for nature conservation in the upper estuary. Arrangements would be needed to preserve the important salmon and trout fishing in the rivers flowing into the estuary. The large catchment is sparsely populated and water stored behind the barrage would be of good quality.

B.70   The main disadvantage of the Solway Firth is that it is so far from the main centres of population and demand. The high cost of conveying water to where it is needed effectively rules it out of consideration within the period of this report.

The Severn (paragraph 221)
B.71   The scheme for which details are set out in Appendix A involves the construction of bunded reservoirs in the inter-tidal area of the estuary known as the Welsh Grounds between the mouths of the rivers Usk and Wye. It is based on a three stage scheme examined in the course of our study of Wales and the Midlands. The scheme has not been investigated in detail but it is apparent that site conditions, including the large tidal range, and the need for long aqueducts for both filling the reservoirs and delivering the stored water, make this an expensive proposal.

Groundwater
Great Ouse (paragraphs 184/185)
B.72   Following the recommendation in our report on the South

East, the river authority have completed a pilot scheme to investigate the possibility that substantial quantities of water might be made available by controlled development of groundwater in the Chalk. The pilot scheme has established the feasibility of development on a large scale and the yield assumed in Appendix A is based on its conclusions. A major consideration in assessing yields is the need to preserve river flows.

B.73   The first stage of the operational scheme is likely to be in the catchment of the river Cam to provide a direct supply to Cambridge, together with an extension of the pilot scheme in the catchment of the Little Ouse. Later stages would involve the Lark, Wissey and Nar catchments, and would be used to augment dry weather flows in the Ely Ouse to allow increased abstractions above Denver.

Thames (paragraphs 184/185)
B.74   The Thames Conservancy's scheme involves the controlled use of groundwater, drawn upon intermittently to augment low river flows. It is based on a pilot scheme carried out during 1967–69 in the Chalk aquifer of the Lambourn valley. The first stage, which has been approved by the Secretary of State, is mainly in the Lambourn and Pang catchments, with some development in the Kennet east of Newbury and in the Loddon south of Reading. Further stages would be in the remainder of the Kennet catchment in west Berkshire and the Marlborough area, and in an area of Jurassic limestones in the Cotswolds west of Oxford.

B.75   The effects of such abstractions on stream flows near to and upstream of the boreholes were studied as part of the pilot scheme. Test pumping resulted in more extended drying out of the bed of the Winterbourne stream than normal. The Conservancy propose to operate the development scheme, however, only in times of drought when intermittent streams are already dry and to continue pumping until the natural base flow returns in the perennial reaches. They consider that this method of operation should not cause any lasting damage to the ecology of the streams.

B.76   We agree generally with this view. In these dry years, however, some intermittent streams would be affected over a longer length and for a longer period. This will temporarily affect the local ecology, although means to mitigate such effects are under development. This will require continuing research as an integral part of the development scheme.

The Trent (paragraphs 41/42; 228; 262–265)
B.77   The river Trent is the third longest river in England and Wales. Its average flow at Nottingham is nearly 7 million cu.m.d. It is therefore a large potential source for water supply and geographically it is well placed to meet demands in the north and east Midlands. In the past the Trent has been badly polluted by domestic and industrial effluents, and while there have been recent improvements in quality doubts remain about its acceptability as a source of potable water supply.

B.78   These problems were investigated in the Trent Research Programme. In our report on this programme we could not recommend that the river Trent should be used as a source for public supply and emphasised the need for further research into the effluent and water treatment processes necessary to achieve specified standards of water quality.

B.79   One possible method of improving the quality of Trent water is to recharge it into the Bunter Sandstone from which water is already abstracted for public water supply. An experimental project within the research programme produced results good enough to justify further work in this direction. Present indications are that water treated in this way would be marginally more expensive than direct abstraction followed by advance water treatment processes. Moreover recharge through a basin system requires a substantial area of land amounting to just under half what would be required for a conventional lowland reservoir producing the same yield.

Appendix C Potential pipeline and tunnel aqueducts

Introduction

C.1 The strategies considered in our report entail extensive use of rivers for conveying water towards the centres of demand. But inevitably man made aqueducts, either pipelines or tunnels, will also be needed as part of the transmission system. Aqueducts will be needed both for conveying water in bulk from source or carrier rivers to deficiency centres for subsequent distribution and for linking river systems together so that water can be transferred from one to another to augment flows as necessary.

Schedules of pipeline and tunnel aqueducts

C.2 The potential pipelines and tunnels considered in the study for our report are listed in Tables C.1–C.3 together with the main assumptions used for costing purposes.

C.3 Table C.1 lists aqueducts required for links between rivers or between rivers and storage in the various programmes within our preferred strategy of mixed inland and estuary storage—(Strategies C and D—see Chapter 8 and Table 16).

C.4 Table C.2 lists aqueducts required in variations of that strategy for links to deficiency centres from sources and rivers and for links between deficiency centres.

C.5 Table C.3 lists other aqueducts considered as possible routes but not included in the preferred strategy.

C.6 Table C.4 gives supplementary information on:

(i) those aqueducts or sections of aqueducts which are assumed to be tunnels; and

(ii) those aqueducts which have been treated and costed as pipelines in the study but where tunnels might be an alternative for at least part of the route for certain of the resource development programmes.

C.7 Factors governing the choice between pipelines and tunnels are set out in paragraphs C.16–36. Several of the aqueduct links may be a combination of pipeline and tunnel and for some the eventual choice is open and would need more detailed investigation of the relative merits of each in the light of a particular programme of source development.

Pipelines

Investigation of Routes

C.8 Not all the routes for aqueducts have been surveyed on the ground. Some proposed aqueducts follow existing routes, or routes proposed in more detailed studies of specific schemes. In other cases routes have been located on maps so as to combine reasonable directness with minimising or, where possible, avoiding obvious difficulties.

Basic Data

C.9 The tables show the assumed location and elevation of the starting and finishing points of the aqueducts, the maximum static pressure (taking into account intermediate high points on the route), and the length.

Required Size and Staging of Pipelines

C.10 The diameter and the number of stages required vary according to the particular programme. Tables C.1 and C.2 show the range required within the programmes of strategies C and D. They have been calculated in each case to give the least combination of capital and pumping costs subject to limitations on maximum velocities of flow and on the number of stages.

C.11 The nominal internal diameters assumed are shown in both inches and millimetres. They may not conform exactly to standard sizes, which for some materials such as steel are based on external diameters. Without pre-judging the pipe material to be used, however, internal diameters are the most meaningful and they can be easily converted to equivalent standard sizes at the design stage of a particular scheme.

C.12 Not more than two stages of construction for pipelines have been considered. More would generally cause greater disturbance along the route than could be justified by deferment of expenditure.

Direction of Flow

C.13 The tables indicate those aqueducts which are intended for use in both directions. They are in two categories. The first are for use in either direction at any given time: from pumping into storage in one direction and for regulation releases in the other. In the second the direction of flow will be one way for some years and will then be reversed following the introduction of a new source and change of the distribution pattern; for example, the proposed Severn–Dee aqueduct is intended for use in the first instance from south to north and in later years from north to south.

Location of Treatment

C.14 The transfer aqueducts in Table C.1 are assumed to convey raw water (apart from settlement in raw water storage and chlorine dosage). The aqueducts to deficiency centres in Table C.2 however are generally assumed to convey fully treated water, so that the problems of bulk movement of raw water are minimised. But there are several exceptions to this: where a deficiency centre is supplied from a combination of sources (including "conjunctive use" sources), the balance of advantage may lie with treating the combined supply at or near the delivery point.

Costs

C.15 Costs adopted for pipelines are as set out in Appendix E, Table E.1. The unit rates for pipelines are based on those used in our studies of the North and of Wales and the Midlands, increased by 75 per cent to cover price increases between 1967 and 1972. Total costs of aqueducts include, where applicable, river intakes, raw water storage, pumping stations and pumping machinery to match the proposed staging of the pipelines. It is envisaged that on long pipelines pumping will be boosted at staging points along the route in order to reduce the maximum pressure.

Tunnels

C.16 We have examined the feasibility of using tunnels where there is a prima facie likelihood that they offer a better or at least a possible alternative to pipelines.

C.17 The factors governing the choice between tunnels and pipelines are:

(i) terrain to be traversed;

(ii) geology on the route;

(iii) quantity of water to be transmitted;

(iv) pressures involved;

these are the four main factors and they affect:

(v) the capital and running costs of tunnels and pipelines;

additional factors are:

(vi) disturbance to the landscape, buildings and services at, or near, ground level;

(vii) security in service, need for maintenance, future need for capacity and life expectancy of works before replacement.

Terrain

C.18 Tunnels offer an advantage in hilly and mountainous areas where substantial savings in pumping costs can be gained by tunnelling through high ground and thus reducing the pumping head. River to river transfers invariably involve crossing high ground between catchments, and with the increasing need for major links between rivers, more tunnels are likely.

C.19 Tunnels may also offer a better solution than pipelines where there are severe obstacles at ground level as in heavily built up areas.

Geology and Construction

C.20 The most important physical factor affecting the use of tunnels is the geology on the proposed route. There are relatively few geological conditions which rule out the use of tunnels, but in certain conditions the cost could be seriously affected.

C.21 Developments in tunnelling by machine in clays and in the associated design of segmental linings have approximately halved costs of clay tunnelling over the last fifteen years, inflation apart. In hard rocks the advances have not been so great, but developments continue in machines and in lining techniques. Progress in engineering geology makes it possible to determine the nature of the strata, particularly its strength and physical properties and to predict the stability of the tunnel and hence to assess the best method of construction and type of lining required. These predictions are complicated in hard rock formations by the presence of jointing, fracturing and flowing water.

C.22 While tunnelling costs have fallen, pipeline costs have increased, mainly due to increases in costs of material such as steel and also to a shortage of skilled pipe layers.

Quantities and Pressure of Water to be Transmitted

C.23 For practical reasons of construction, tunnels are not normally built less than about 2 m in diameter; usually they are between 2·5–3·0 m in diameter. Thus the minimum size of tunnels is about the same as the maximum size of pipelines. A tunnel can only be justified economically where the quantities of water require a large diameter aqueduct. It is not necessary for the quantity to be greater than that carried by a large pipe, because in some conditions a tunnel will be cheaper than a smaller size pipeline but in general a tunnel would not be justified for an aqueduct of less than 1·7 m.

C.24 Sometimes the choice may be between a single tunnel and two pipelines in parallel, laid in stages as demands and hence the quantities of water to be conveyed grow.

C.25 Tunnels may be required to withstand either gravity pressures limited to the amount required to overcome hydraulic friction or the combined pumping pressure required to overcome static and friction head. Pressure tunnels are inevitably more expensive than those subject only to atmospheric pressure and if very high pressures are involved, pipelines may well be a better choice. In some cases an appropriate arrangement may be the use of pipelines over any sections requiring high pressure pumping, confining tunnels to the low pressure sections.

C.26 It is necessary to make an economic comparison of the options in each case.

Disturbance during Construction

C.27 In many heavily developed urban areas or other areas of intensive land use the disruption and damage caused by construction of large pipelines would be highly objectionable, if not altogether un-acceptable. Such areas are difficult to avoid altogether as they occur around centres of heavy demand to which aqueducts must be provided. Where conditions are suitable, tunnelling may offer an attractive and economical solution to this problem. In rural areas too, tunnelling may prove increasingly attractive as concern grows about the effects on the countryside of laying large pipes. This would be particularly so if the disturbance had to be repeated because the pipeline was constructed in stages in order to match the timing of capital expenditure to the rate of growth of demand.

C.28 A tunnel causes no such disturbance along its route, although there may be difficulty in disposing of large volumes of excavated materials at the terminal points or at any intermediate shafts. This difficulty is likely to occur only once in many years, however, as the large carrying capacity of tunnels and the relationship between cost and carrying capacity are such that we foresee no case within the time scale of the study where there would be an advantage in staging a tunnel.

Security and Life of Tunnel Works

C.29 Any appraisal between tunnels and pipelines must consider the relative security in service and length of life of the works before major maintenance or renewal is needed.

C.30 A tunnel probably gives greater security than a pipeline against accidental or deliberate fracture or damage. If, however, a pipeline were duplicated or triplicated, it is arguable that the security thus afforded to maintenance of supplies would be at least equivalent to that of a single tunnel.

C.31 The life of tunnel works before the need for replacement is considerably greater than that of pipelines, as reflected by the accepted loan repayment periods of 60 years for tunnels and 30 or 40 years, according to size, for pipelines.

Potential Tunnels

C.32 Table C.4 lists those aqueducts (included in Tables C.1, C.2 and C.3) which are potentially suitable for tunnels. The list takes into account the appropriate economic, operational and amenity advantage that may result from the use of tunnels rather than pipelines. The first part of the table lists those routes where we consider a tunnel likely; the second part lists other routes which have been assumed to be pipelines but where tunnels may be an alternative for at least part of the route. A desk study of the feasibility of tunnelling on each of these links has been made either by consulting engineers or by our staff. In some cases the work is more advanced and site investigations have been undertaken and detailed designs prepared.

C.33 The tunnel links shown in Table C.4 fall into four distinct categories:

(i) *Stiff homogeneous clays* Tunnelling by machine. Continuous permanent lining will be required.

(ii) *Uniform sandstone and limestone with high rates of water inflow* Tunnelling by machine may be possible on this type of strata and permanent linings will be required.

(iii) *Hard intact or fractured sedimentary or igneous rocks* Inflow of water may occur locally on fault lines or in highly jointed or fractured zones, but is unlikely to present a constant problem. A mixed driving face of hard and soft strata may be encountered and this, together with jointing and fracturing, may preclude the use of tunnelling machines. Traditional drill and blast methods will mostly be used but the speed and cost of drilling may be improved by advances in metallurgy. Temporary support during driving may only be required locally and a permanent lining other than in badly fractured sections may only be needed to improve the hydraulic efficiency.

(iv) *Unconsolidated sands and clays* Tunnelling in these materials may only be necessary for relatively short lengths at the tunnel portals. Such tunnelling is difficult, unpredictable and expensive and should, if possible, be avoided. However, new methods under full scale test may greatly improve the prospects in such materials.

C.34 The total lengths of potential tunnel links listed in Table C.4 which fall into the first three categories are as follows:

Table C.5

	Category of Strata	Potential length of tunnel —km
(i)	Stiff homogeneous clays	182
(ii)	Uniform sandstone and limestone with high rates of water inflow	58
(iii)	Hard intact or fractured sedimentary or igneous rocks	210

C.35 In some of the proposed clay tunnels the depth of overburden may be up to three times that for water supply tunnels driven in this material in the United Kingdom in the past. This may cause problems in lining design, but with the continuing improvements in this well-established and highly mechanised technique these difficulties should be overcome. Tunnelling methods in medium to hard rocks are not so advanced and in view of likely tunnelling in future in such strata there is an obvious need for field research. For this reason we are collaborating with the Northumbrian River Authority and the Building Research Station in driving a number of experimental headings in the Carboniferous formations of the northern Pennines to examine tunnelling problems in advance of the proposed construction of the Tyne–Tees tunnel. The results of these experiments will be applicable both to the construction of that tunnel and to others constructed in similar difficult conditions of variable hardness.

Table C.1
Aqueduct Schedule—New Aqueducts for River to River and River to Storage transfers included in variations of preferred strategy

Ref No	Starting point	Ending point	D=direct supply R=regulating F=filling	P=pipe T=tunnel	Grid reference Start	Grid reference End	Elevation metres AOD Start	Elevation metres AOD End	Summit Elevation m	Summit Distance from start km	Static head difference m	Overall length km	Assumed number of stages/range of nominal internal diameters of new pipes (in)	(mm)	Remarks	References in Table C.4
101	Tyne at Riding Mill	Airy Holm tunnel portal	R	P	NZ0261	NZ0455	15	228			+213	6	2/54–2/66	2/1375–2/1675		
102	Airy Holm tunnel portal	Wear at Stanhope	R	T	NZ0455	NZ0137	229	202			−27	19	—	—	—	401
103	Wear at Stanhope	Tees at Eggleston	R	T	NZ0137	NZ0022	202	183			−19	14	—	-	—	402
104	Tees at Stapleton	Swale	R	P	NZ2711	SE2499	30	55	74	6	+44	14	2/27–1/72	2/675–1/1825		
105	Yorks Ouse at Skelton	Wharfe at Cawood	R	P	SE5555	SE5638	11	6	30	8	+19	17	2/39–2/60	2/1000–2/1525	Initial spare capacity in existing aqueduct =45 thousand cu.m.d	
106	Wharfe at Cawood	Yorks Derwent at Barmby	R	P	SE5638	SE6829	6	6	12	6	+6	16	2/39–1/69	2/1000–1/1750		
107	Eden at Staingills	Haweswater reservoir	F	P	NY5831	NY5015	87	276			+189	21	2/60–2/69	2/1525–2/1750		
108	Haweswater reservoir	Birk Beck	R	T	NY4915	NY5907	212	200			−12	12	—	—	Birk Beck is a tributary of the Lune	403
109	Lune at Borrow Beck confluence	Borrowbeck reservoir	F	P	NY6101	NY5901	146	274			+128	2	1/63	1/1600		
110	Lune at Sedburgh	Garsdale	R	P	SD6392	SD7690	99	250			+151	13	1/69	1/1750	Aqueduct Ref Nos 110 and 111 comprise the Upper Lune to Yorkshire Ouse transfer link	
111	Garsdale tunnel	Ure at Bainbridge	R	T and P	SD7690	SD9390	250	205			−45	18	1/63	1/600	Includes 8 km of pipeline	404
112	Morecambe Bay (Carnforth)	Lune near Aughton	R/D	T and P	SD4871	SD5566	9	30			+21	9	2/66–3/66*	2/1675–3/1675*	Includes 4 km of pipeline *2 pipes may form 1 stage	405
113	Lune near Aughton	Ribble downstream of Settle	R	T and P	SD5566	SD8062	12	130			+118	25	—	—	Includes short length of pipeline	406
114	Lune near Halton	Wyre at Abbeystead	D/R	T and P	SD5164	SD5553	12	122			+110	12	2/60–2/72	2/1525–2/1825	Includes 6 km of pipeline	407, 408
115	Ribble at Hellifield	Wharfe at Bolton Abbey	R	P	SD8356	SE0753	122	95	162	22	+40	26	1/60–2/72	1/1525–2/1825	Alternative tunnel given in Table C.4 Group II	422, 423
116	Dee Estuary	Dee at Chester	R	P	SJ2972	SJ4164	6	6			0	16	1/63	1/1600		
117	Dee at Chester	Dee at Coed-yr-Allt	R	P	SJ4164	SJ3239	6	40	107	25	+101	27	1/21–1/36	1/525–1/925		
118	Dee at Chester	Churnet at Cheddleton	R	P	SJ4164	SJ9852	6	140	168	60	+162	71	1/69	1/1750	Costs included-allow for channel improvements on Churnet (a tributary of the Trent) downstream of Cheddleton	
119	Craig Goch reservoir	Wye at Pont-yr-Marteg	R/F	T	SN9071	SN9571	317to 374	217			−100 or +157	5	—	—	Flow is reversible	412
120	Wye at Pont-yr-Marteg	Dulas at Craigtylwch	R/F	T	SN9571	SN9680	217	210			−7	10	—	—	Flow is reversible	413
121	Tanat	Vyrnwy reservoir	F	P	SJ0825	SJ0120	140	275	310	5	+170	10	1/60	1/1525		
122	Severn at Melverley	Dee at Coed-yr-Allt	R	P	SJ3417	SJ3239	55	40	99	18	+44	23	1/30–2/45	1/750–2/1150	Flow is reversible but if transfers are only northwards SJ3138 is an alternative end. Tunnel alternative given in Table C.4 Group II	426

Table C.1 continued

Aqueduct Schedule—New Aqueducts for River to River and River to Storage transfers included in variations of preferred strategy

Ref No	Starting point	Ending point	D=direct supply / R=regulating / F=filling	P=pipe / T=tunnel	Grid reference Start	Grid reference End	Elevation metres AOD Start	Elevation metres AOD End	Summit Elevation m	Summit Distance from start km	Static head difference m	Overall length km	Stages/range of nominal internal diameters in	Stages/range of nominal internal diameters mm	Remarks	References in Table C.4
123	Severn at Sutton Wood	Dove downstream of Uttoxeter	R	P	SJ7001	SK1231	35	69	122	48	+ 87	52	1/72	1/1825	Tunnel alternative given in Table C.4 Group II	427
124	Dove near Ashbourne	Carsington reservoir	F/R	P	SK1646	SK2450	107	198			+ 92	10	66	1675	Flow is reversible	
125	Dove at Egginton	Aston/Sinfin Moor reservoirs	D/F	P	SK2627	SK3829	46	56	59	7	+ 13	13	2/30–2/66	2/750–2/1675	Comprises part of Dove to Nottingham aqueduct via 126 and 222	
126	Aston/Sinfin Moor reservoirs	Derwent at Church Wilne	D/F	P	SK3829	SK4331	56	32	61	1	+ 5 or 29	6	2/27–2/66	2/675–2/1675	Used as filling aqueduct from Derwent to reservoirs in reverse direction	
127	Trent at Dunham	Bunter recharge	F	P	SK8276	SK6281	3	37			+ 34	20	2/63	2/1600	Notional location given for Bunter re-charge	
128	Severn at Upton	Longdon Marsh reservoir	F/R	P	SO8538	SO8337	11	32			+ 21	3	2/57	2/1450	Flow is reversible	
129	Severn at Wainlode	Dowdeswell tunnel	R	P and T	SO8425	SP0019	8	114	117	11	+109	17	2/48–2/57	2/1225–2/1450	Link 129 includes 15 km of pipeline	415
130	Dowdeswell	Fairford Ponds	R	T	SP0019	SU1799	114	76			− 38	26	—	—	Links 129–133 inclusive comprise the Severn to Thames transfer system	416
131	Fairford Ponds	Thames at Buscot	R	P	SU1899	SU2398	76	68			− 8	5	2/60–2/66	2/1525–2/1675		
132	Buscot	Thames at Appleton	R	P	SU2398	SP4201	69	63	75	17	+ 6	20	1/50–1/100	1/1300–1/2550		
133	Appleton	Thames at Abingdon	R	P	SP4201	SU4995	63	50	75	1	+ 12	10	1/33–1/63	1/850–1/1600		
134	Brianne reservoir	Irfon	R	T	SN8150	SN8549	243	220			− 23	5	—	—	Irfon is a tributary of the Wye	414
135	Wye at Ross	Severn at Wainlode	R	P	SO5925	SO8425	34	8	98	7	+ 64	26	1/48–1/54	1/1225–1/1375		
136	Wye at Bigsweir	Sharpness canal at Sharpness	R	P	SO5305	SO6702	12	6	208	4	+196	14	1/48–1/54	1/1225–1/1375	More detailed study would probably result in the inclusion of a length of tunnel	
137	Wye at Monmouth	Usk at Usk	R	P	SO5111	SO3700	15	10	72	9	+ 57	21	2/33–2/36	2/850–2/925		
138	Thames upstream of Oxford	Otmoor	F/R	T	SP4710	SP5513	59	76 to 60			+ 17 to − 1	8	—	—	Flow is reversible	417, 418
139	Thames at Hampton	Lockwood shaft	R	T	TQ1369	TQ3589	6	8			+ 2	31	(100)	—	Existing tunnel with 340 thousand cu.m.d initial spare capacity	
140	Cut-off channel at Blackdyke	Kennet pumping station	R	T	TL6988	TL7068	0	−26			− 26	20	(100)	—	Existing tunnel with 800 thousand cu.m.d initial spare capacity	
141	Kennet pumping station	Stour (Essex) at Kirtling Green	R	P	TL7068	TL6856	−26	107			+ 133	14	(72)	—	Existing pipeline with 340 thousand cu.m.d initial spare capacity	
142	Stour (Essex) at Wixoe	Pant at Great Sampford	R	P	TL7143	TL6435	51	67	113	6	+ 62	11	1/45	1/1150	Initial spare capacity of existing 60" pipe is 280 thousand cu.m.d. The diameters shown refer to a new aqueduct	

Table C.1 continued

Aqueduct Schedule—New Aqueducts for River to River and River to Storage transfers included in variations of preferred strategy

Ref No	Starting point	Ending point	D=direct supply R=regulating F=filling	P=pipe T=tunnel	Grid reference Start	End	Elevation metres AOD Start	End	Summit Elevation m	Summit Distance from start km	Static head difference m	Overall length km	Assumed number of stages/range of nominal internal diameters of new pipes in	mm	Remarks	References in Table C.4
143	Cut-off channel at Denver	Old Bedford river	D	P	TF5900	TL5698	0	0			0	5	2/66	2/1675		429
144	Old Bedford river	Earith	D	P	TL5698	TL3974	0	0			0	29	1/72	1/1825	It has been assumed that up to 225 thousand cu.m.d can be transmitted via the ponded Old Bedford river and that this pipeline will be used for additional quantities	429
145	Earith	Brownshill	D/F	P	TL3974	TL3772	0	3			+ 3	3	2/66	2/1675		429
146	Brownshill	Offord	D/F	P	TL3772	TL2166	3	11			+ 8	19	—	—	Initial spare capacity of commissioned aqueduct =800 thousand cu.m.d	429
147	Offord	Grafham Water	F	P	TL2166	TL1766	11	44			+ 33	4	2/54	—	Initial spare capacity of commissioned aqueducts =330 thousand cu.m.d. Tunnel alternative to links 143 to 147 inclusive given in Table C.4 Group II	429
148	Nene at Wansford	Welland at Tinwell	R	P	TL0799	TF0106	8	23	52	6	+ 44	10	1/21	1/525		

Table C.2
Aqueduct Schedule—New Aqueducts to Notional Deficiency centres included in variations of preferred strategy

Ref No	Starting point	Ending point	D=direct supply R=regulating F=filling	P=pipe T=tunnel	Grid reference Start	Grid reference End	Elevation metres AOD Start	Elevation metres AOD End	Summit Elevation m	Summit Distance from start km	Static head difference m	Overall length km	Assumed stages/diameters in	Assumed stages/diameters mm	Remarks	References in Table C.4
201	Tyne at Wylam	NEWCASTLE	D	P	NZ1064	NZ2169	15	122			+107	13	2/39	2/1000		
202	Wear at Finchale Priory	SUNDERLAND	D	P	NZ2947	NZ3250	15	122			+107	4	2/33	2/850		
203	Tees at Low Worsall	TEESSIDE	D	P	NZ3811	NZ3720	6	91			+85	9	2/51	2/1300		
204	Barmby	HULL	D	P	SE6829	SE9929	0	76			+76	32	2/24	2/600		
205	Barmby	HUMBERSIDE	D	P	SE6829	TA0107	0	76			+76	41	2/39	2/1000		
206	Wharfe at Cawood	SHEFFIELD/CHESTERFIELD	D	P	SE5638	SK4179	6	152			+146	63	1/30-2/45	1/750 -2/1150	Initial spare capacity of existing aqueduct =45 thousand cu.m.d	
207	Wharfe at Cawood	WEST RIDING NORTH	D	P	SE5638	SE2428	6	168			+162	35	2/36	2/925		
208	Wharfe at Boston Spa	WEST RIDING NORTH	D	P	SE4246	SE2428	13	168			+153	35	2/36-1/39	2/925 -1/1000		
209	Derwent (Cumberland)	WEST CUMBERLAND	D	P	NY0129	NY0022	6	107			+101	8	2/24	2/600		
210	Wyre at Abbeystead	FYLDE/PRESTON	D	T and P	SD5553	SD6137	107	137			+30	17	2/60-2/72	2/1525-2/1825	Includes 3 km of pipeline	409, 410
211	Ribble at Mitton	FYLDE/PRESTON	D	P	SD7137	SD6137	38	137			+99	10	2/36-2/51	2/925 -2/1300		
212	FYLDE/PRESTON	Lostock	D	P	SD6137	SD6509	137	110			-27	31	1/48-1/72.	1/1225-1/1825	See tunnel alternative for part of this link in Table C.4 Group II	424
213	Horwich	Rivington	F/D	P	SD6211	SD6312	110	142			+32	1	1/42-1/51	1/1075-1/1300	Flow direction is reversible	
214	Lostock	LIVERPOOL	D	P	SD6509	SJ4793	110	84	134	2	+24	24	1/45-2/60	1/1150-2/1525		
215	Lostock	MANCHESTER	D	P	SD6509	SJ7995	110	110			0	20	1/42-1/54	1/1075-1/1375		
216	Dee at Chester	LIVERPOOL	D	P	SJ4164	SJ4793	6	84			+78	36	1/21-1/36	1/525 -1/925	Initial spare capacity of existing aqueduct =340 thousand cu.m.d. Tunnel alternative from the Dee Estuary is given in Table C.4 Group II	425
217	LIVERPOOL	MANCHESTER	D	P	SJ4793	SJ7995	84	110			+26	34	1/36-2/48	1/925 -2/1225		
218	Dove above Uttoxeter	STOKE	D	P	SK1034	SJ8439	70	213			+143	27	2/33	2/850		
219	Dove at Egginton	LEICESTER	D	P	SK2627	SK5311	46	143			+97	34	2/36-1/39	2/925 -1/1000		
220	Derwent at Church Wilne	LEICESTER	D	P	SK4331	SK5311	32	143			+111	23	1/39-1/45	1/1000-1/1150		
221	Wing	LEICESTER	D	P	SK8902	SK5311	124	143	169	11	+45	37	1/18	1/450		
222	Derwent at Church Wilne	NOTTINGHAM	D	P	SK4331	SK4537	32	140			±108	7	2/33-2/45	2/850 -2/1150		
223	Derwent at Church Wilne	SHEFFIELD/CHESTERFIELD	D	P	SK4331	SK4179	32	152			+120	50	1/24-1/45	1/600 -1/1150		
224	Bunter recharge	SHEFFIELD/CHESTERFIELD	D	P	SK6281	SK4179	37	152			+115	22	1/66-1/72	1/1675-1/1825		
225	Bunter recharge	NOTTINGHAM	D	P	SK6281	SK4537	37	140			+103	47	51-54	1300-1375		
226	Severn at Sutton Wood	STOKE	D	P	SJ7001	SJ8439	35	213			+178	42	2/36	2/925		

Table C.2 continued

Aqueduct Schedule—New Aqueducts to Notional Deficiency centres included in variations of preferred strategy

Ref No	Starting point	Ending point	D=direct supply / R=regulating / F=filling	P=pipe / T=tunnel	Grid reference Start	Grid reference End	Elevation metres AOD Start	Elevation metres AOD End	Summit Elevation m	Summit Distance from start km	Static head difference m	Overall length km	Assumed stages/diameters in	Assumed stages/diameters mm	Remarks	References in Table C.4
227	Severn at Hampton Loade	BIRMINGHAM	D	P	SO7486	SO9291	23	229			+ 206	20	2/60-2/63	2/1525-2/1600		
228	Severn at Worcester	WORCESTER	D	P	SO8459	SO8960	11	114			+ 103	5	2/33	2/850		
229	Severn at Upton	COVENTRY	D	P	SO8538	SP4278	11	94			+ 83	72	2/27-2/36	2/675 -2/925	Tunnel alternative given in Table C.4 Group II	428
230	COVENTRY	NORTHAMPTON	D	P	SP4278	SP8271	94	143	177	22	+ 83	42	2/24-1/39	2/600 -1/1000		
231	Wing (Empingham treatment works)	NORTHAMPTON	D	P	SK8902	SP8271	124	143			+ 19	32	1/54	1/1375	Initial spare capacity of existing aqueduct =270 thousand cu.m.d	
232	Grafham Water	Great Doddington	D	P	TL1665	SP8864	38	100			+ 62	28	1/18-1/63	1/450 -1/1600	Initial spare capacity of existing aqueduct =80 thousand cu.m.d	
233	Great Doddington	BUCKS	D	P	SP8864	SP8129	100	152			+ 52	35	1/27-1/30	1/675 -1/750		
234	Great Doddington	NORTHAMPTON	D	P	SP8864	SP8271	100	143			+ 43	10	1/18-1/63	1/450 -1/1600	Initial spare capacity of existing aqueduct =80 thousand cu.m.d	
235	Severn at Gloucester	GLOUCESTER	D	P	SO8220	SO8819	6	122			+ 116	7	2/30-2/33	2/750 -2/850		
236	Sharpness canal at Sharpness	BRISTOL	D	P	SO6702	ST6177	6	122			+ 116	26	2/42	2/1075		
237	Usk at Llantrisant	CARDIFF	D	P	ST3896	ST2084	8	114			+ 106	24	2/42	2/1075		
238	Trent at Dunham	HUMBERSIDE	D	P	SK8276	TA0107	3	76			+ 73	37	1/24	1/600		
239	Silsoe	BEDS AND HUNTS	D	P	TL0835	TL0439	55	126			+ 71	6	1/27-1/39	1/675 -1/1000		
240	Grafham Water	BEDS AND HUNTS	D	P	TL1665	TL0439	38	126			+ 88	30	2/30-2/36	2/1750-2/925	Initial spare capacity of existing aqueduct =180 thousand cu.m.d	
241	Thames near Oxford	OXFORD	D	P	SP4710	SP4506	59	122			+ 63	5	1/30-1/33	1/750 -1/850		
242	Otmoor	BUCKS	D	P	SP5915	SP8129	60	152			+ 92	27	1/45-1/48	1/1150-1/1225		
243	BEDS AND HUNTS	BUCKS	D	P	TL0439	SP8129	126	152			+ 26	25	1/42	1/1075	Initial spare capacity of existing aqueduct =45 thousand cu.m.d	
244	Thames	THAMES	D	P	Variable	Variable	15	122			+ 107	16	2/54	2/1375	Notional link	
245	Thames at Sunnymead	COLNE	D	P	SU9975	TR1586	14	116			+ 102	20	1/30-2/33	1/1750-2/850	Initial spare capacity of existing aqueduct =80 thousand cu.m.d	
246	Beds and Hunts	UPPER LEE	D	P	TL0439	TL2717	126	125			− 1	32	1/30	1/750	Initial spare capacity of existing aqueduct =55 thousand cu.m.d	
247	Thames at Sunnymead	UPPER LEE	D	P	SU9975	TL2717	14	125			+ 111	55	1/27-1/39	1/675 -1/1000		
248	Lockwood	LONDON	D	P	TQ3589	TQ3182	8	76			+ 68	8	1/51	1/1300		
249	Thames at Hampton	LONDON	D	P	TQ1369	TQ3182	6	76			+ 70	24	1/39-2/42	1/1000-2/1075		

Table C.2 continued

Aqueduct Schedule—New Aqueducts to Notional Deficiency centres included in variations of preferred strategy

Ref No	Starting point	Ending point	D=direct supply R=regulating F=filling	P=pipe T=tunnel	Grid reference Start	Grid reference End	Elevation metres AOD Start	Elevation metres AOD End	Summit Elevation m	Summit Distance from start km	Static head difference m	Overall length km	Assumed number of stages/range of nominal internal diameters of new pipes in	mm	Remarks	References in Table C.4
250	Lockwood	SOUTH ESSEX	D	P	TQ3589	TQ6391	8	79	100	17	+ 92	30	1/30–2/45	1/750 –2/1150	Initial spare capacity of existing aqueduct =90 thousand cu.m.d	
251	Blackwater at Langford	SOUTH ESSEX	D	P	TL8309	TQ6391	3	79			+ 76	27	1/36–2/48	1/925 –2/1225	Initial spare capacity of existing aqueduct =55 thousand cu.m.d	
252	Stour near Colchester	NORTH ESSEX	D	P	TM0134	TM0233	9	76			+ 67	2	2/27–2/30	2/675 –2/750	Initial spare capacity of existing aqueduct =55 thousand cu.m.d	
253	Great Ouse Groundwater	CAMBRIDGE	D	P	Variable	TL4954	91	61			– 30	18	2/36	2/925		
254	Welland near Stamford	SOUTH LINCS	D	P	TF0907	TF1001	9	53			+ 44	6	2/24	2/600		
255	Cut-off channel at Denver	TIDAL OUSE	D	P	TF5900	TF6715	0	40			+ 40	16	2/27	2/675		

Table C.3
Aqueduct Schedule—New Aqueducts included only in Integrated Programmes outside preferred strategy

Ref No	Starting point	Ending point	D=direct supply / R=regulating / F=filling	P=pipe / T=tunnel	Grid reference Start	Grid reference End	Elevation metres AOD Start	Elevation metres AOD End	Summit Elevation m	Summit Distance from start km	Static head difference m	Overall length km	Remarks	References in Table C.4
301	Solway at Bowness	Greenhead	R	P	NY2262	NY6466	6	146			+ 140	46	For tunnel alternative to parts of 301 and 302 see Table C.4 Group II	421
302	Greenhead	South Tyne at Haltwhistle	R	P	NY6466	NY6963	146	113			− 33	6		
303	MANCHESTER	Churnet at Cheddleton	R	P	SJ7995	SJ9852	110	140	168	49	+ 58	60	See note for Ref No 118	
304	Dee at Corwen	Alwen at Cefn-Post	F	P	SJ0744	SJ0049	131	260			+ 129	11	Aqueducts 304 and 305 required for a larger Brenig reservoir development with pumped filling as variation B in Table A1	
305	Afon Alwen at Cefn-Post	Brenig reservoir	F	P	SJ0049	SH9854	260	398			+ 138	6		
306	Afon Banwy	Gam reservoir	F	P	SJ0410	SH9807	152	275			+ 123	9		
307	Nant-y-Moch reservoir	Biga	R	T	SN7788	SN8689	326	292			− 34	9	Biga is a tributary of the Severn	411
308	Wye at Chepstow	Sharpness canal at Sharpness	R	P	ST5393	SO6702	9	6	15	10	+ 6	18	Relates to Severn Estuary storage filled from the Wye given in Table A.4. Enables this source to supply Bristol	
309	Sharpness canal at Woolstrop	Leckhampton	R	P	SO8015	SO9419	6	117			+ 111	15	Connects to Severn—Thames transfer link at Leckhampton	415, 416
310	Severn upstream of Welshpool	Marton Pool reservoir	F/R	P	SJ2101	SJ2802	67	104 to 130			+ 63 or − 37	9	Flow is reversible	
311	Severn at Upton	Oxford canal near the tunnel	R	P	SO8640	SP4551	11	114	128	64	+ 117	66	Route is common to the Upton–Coventry link 229 as far as Bidford on Avon. For tunnel alternative see Table C.4 Group II	428
312	Oxford canal at Kings Sutton	Great Ouse downstream of Buckingham	R	P	SP4934	SP7234	79	75	134	9	+ 55	23	Costs allow for improvement works on Great Ouse downstream of Buckingham	
313	LEICESTER	NORTHAMPTON	D	P	SK5311	SP8271	144	144	168	29	+ 24	54		
314	COVENTRY	LEICESTER	D	P	SP4278	SK5311	94	144			+ 50	34		
315	Thames at Marlow	Whitchurch and/or Waddesdon reservoirs	F/R	T	SU8786	SP8220 and/or SP7112	24	Whitchurch 90 to 122 Waddesdon 70 to 107			+ 98 or − 66; + 83 or − 46	30 to 45*	Flow is reversible. See also Table C.4 Group 1. *Alignment and length of tunnels depends on whether one or both reservoirs is constructed and, if both, order of construction	419
316	Lockwood shaft	Cobbins Brook reservoir	F/D	T	TQ3589	TL4202	8	73			+ 65	14	See also Table C.4 Group I	420
317	Cobbins Brook reservoir	UPPER LEE	D	P	TL4202	TL2717	40	125			+ 85	21		
318	Cobbins Brook reservoir	SOUTH ESSEX	D	P	TL4202	TQ6391	40	79	100	15	+ 60	27		
319	Pant at Great Sampford	Stort at Clavering	R	P	TL6435	TL4731	67	88	117	8	+ 50	17		
320	Stort near Roydon	UPPER LEE	D	P	TL3910	TL2717	31	125			+ 94	14		
321	Old Bedford at Earith	Silsoe	D	P	TL3974	TL0835	0	55			+ 55	49		
322	Silsoe	Thame near Wheatley	R	P	TL0835	SP6104	55	55	116	12	+ 61	57		
323	Bedford Ouse at Kempston	BEDS AND HUNTS	D	P	TL0147	TL0439	27	126			+ 99	9		

Table C.4
Tunnel Schedule—Group I—Aqueducts assumed to be Tunnels

Complete aqueduct route (From)	(To)	Tunnel sections (Ref No)	Terminal points and national grid references (Start)	(End)	Approximate levels at terminal points metres AOD (Start)	(End)	D=direct supply R=regulating F=filling	Minimum fall through gravity sections (−) or maximum static head on pressure sections (+) metres	Length km	Nominal diameter metres	Typical depth of cover metres	Summary of strata	Remarks	References in Tables C.1, C.2 and C.3
Tyne	Wear and Tees	401	Airy Holm NZ 04 55	Wear at Stanhope NZ 01 37	229	202	R	− 27	19	2·9	130	Carboniferous Limestone series		102
		402	Wear at Stanhope NZ 01 37	Tees at Eggleston NZ 00 22	202	183	R	− 19	14	2·9	220			103
Haweswater	Lune	403	Haweswater NY 49 15	Birk Beck, tributary of Lune NY 59 07	212	200	R	− 12	12	3·4	130	Borrowdale Volcanics and Silurian flags and slates		108
Lune	Yorkshire Ouse	404	Garsdale SD 76 90	Ure, tributary of Ouse, at Apperset SD 88 90	250	230	R	− 20	10	2·4	200	Carboniferous Limestone series		111
Morecambe Bay	Yorkshire Ouse, via Ribble	405	Carnforth SD 51 70	Lune near Aughton SD 55 66	30	30	R	0	5	2·4 to 2·6	100	Carboniferous Limestone and grits with subsidiary shales	Beyond Ribble, link may include tunnel sections; see under Group II tunnels	112
		406	Claughton near Lune SD 56 66	Ribble near Settle SD 80 62	12	130	R	+ 118	25	2·4 to 2·6	130			113
Lune	FYLDE/ PRESTON	407	Lune near Halton SD 51 64	Quernmore Park SD 51 64	12	60	D/R	+ 48	Short Length	3·0	40		For extension of this route to Manchester, see under Group II tunnels	114
		408	Near Quernmore village SD 52 59	Wyre at Abbeystead (North) SD 55 53	107	122	D/R	+ 62* (See under Remarks)	7	2·6	90		*Static head on continuous pressure system, from Quernmore Park to Abbeystead, of which this tunnel constitutes only a part	
		409	Wyre at Abbeystead (South) SD 55 53	Crow Trees SD 60 41	107	124	D	+ 17	13	2·7	150	Carboniferous shales and grits		210
		410	Billington SD 61 38	FYLDE/ PRESTON demand centre SD 61 37	122	137	D	+ 15	1	2·7	20			
Nant-y-Moch reservoir	Severn via Clywedog	411	Nant-y-Moch reservoir SN 77 88	Biga, tributary of Clywedog SN 86 89	326	292	R	− 34	9	2·4	280	Ordovician and Silurian strata		307
Craig Goch reservoir	Upper Wye	412	Craig Goch reservoir SN 90 71	Wye at Pont-yr-Marteg SN 95 71	317 to 374	217	R/F	−100 or +157	5	2·4	150	Ordovician and Silurian strata	Flow is reversible	119
Upper Wye	Upper Severn	413	Wye at Pont-yr-Marteg SN 95 71	Dulas, Severn tributary at Craigtylwch SN 96 80	217	210	R/F	− 7 or + 7	10	2·4	150	Ordovician and Silurian strata	Flow is reversible	120
Llyn Brianne	Upper Wye	414	Llyn Brianne SN 81 50	Irfon, Wye tributary SN 85 49	243	220	R	− 23	5	2·4	240	Ordovician and Silurian strata		134

Table C.4 continued
Tunnel Schedule—Group I—Aqueducts assumed to be Tunnels

Complete aqueduct route		Tunnel sections			D=direct supply R=regulating F=filling	Approximate levels at terminal points metres AOD		Minimum fall through gravity sections (—) or maximum static head on pressure sections (+) metres	Length km	Nominal diameter metres	Typical depth of cover metres	Summary of strata	Remarks	References in Tables C.1, C.2 and C.3
From	To	Ref No	Terminal points and national grid references Start	End		Start	End							
Severn	Thames	415	Leckhampton south of Cheltenham SO 94 19	Lilley Brook SO 96 19	R	117	114	— 3	2	2·8	40	Lias Clay		129
		416	Dowdeswell, SE of Cheltenham SP 00 19	Fairford, NW of Lechlade SU 17 99	R	114	76	— 38	26	2·8	100	Lias Clay and Fullers Earth		130
Thames	Otmoor reservoir	417	Thames at Kings Weir SP 47 10	Cherwell intake SP 52 10	F/R	59	—	+ 17 or — 1	4	3·1	Nominal	Oxford Clay	These two tunnels, together with an inlet/outlet tower and filling/supplying pumps at Otmoor, form a single hydraulic system, capable of operation for either direction of flow	138
		418	Cherwell intake SP 52 10	Otmoor reservoir SP 55 13	F/R	—	60 to 76		4	3·1				
Thames	Whitchurch and/or Waddesdon reservoir	419	Marlow on Thames SU 87 86	Whitchurch or Waddesdon reservoir SP 82 20 or SP 71 12	F/R	24	Whit-church 90 to 122 Wad-desdon 70 to 107	Whitchurch + 98 or — 66 Waddesdon + 83 or — 46	30 to 45* (See under Remarks)	2·5	120	Chalk, Marl, Gault Clay, Kimmeridge Clay	Flow is reversible. *Alignment and length of tunnel depends on whether one or both reservoirs constructed and, if the latter, order of construction	315
Thames	Cobbins Brook reservoir	420	Lockwood shaft TQ 35 89	Cobbins Brook reservoir TL 42 02	F/D	8	73	+ 65	14	2·5	30	London Clay		316

Table C.4 continued

Tunnel Schedule—Group II—Aqueducts costed as Pipelines but where Tunnels might be an alternative

Complete aqueduct route From	To	Tunnel sections Ref No	Terminal points and national grid references Start	End	D=direct supply R=regu-lating F=filling	Approximate levels at terminal points metres AOD Start	End	Minimum fall through gravity sections (—) or maximum static head on pressure sections (+) metres	Length km	Nominal diameter metres	Typical depth of cover metres	Summary of strata	Remarks	References in Tables C.1, C.2 and C.3
Solway Firth	Tyne	421	Irthing valley near Brampton NY 56 63	South Tyne above Haltwhistle NY 67 61	R	75	150	+ 75	11	2·8	100	Carboniferous Limestone series and Coal Measures		301, 302
Morecambe Bay	Yorkshire Ouse, via Ribble, Aire and Wharfe	422	Ribble near Hellifield SD 85 55	Aire near Cargrove SD 91 54	R	120	120	0	6	2·4 to 3·2	110	Carboniferous shales	For tunnels in Morecambe Bay to Ribble section, see under Group I tunnels	115
		423	Aire at Keighley SE 06 43	Wharfe near Ilkley SE 09 48	R	84	76	— 8	6	2·4 to 2·6	210	Carboniferous Limestone and grits with subsidiary shales		115
FYLDE/ PRESTON	MANCHESTER	424	White Coppice, north of Rivington reservoirs SD 61 18	Near Horwich SD 65 11	D	154	146	— 8	9	2·4	110	Carboniferous shales and grits and Coal Measures	Pipelines 212 and 215 would require re-routing on either side of this tunnel if adopted	212
Dee Estuary	LIVERPOOL	425	Dee Estuary SJ 29 72	Liverpool deficiency centre SJ 47 93	D	6	84	+ 78	27	2·4	40	Triassic Sandstone 24 km. Coal Measures 3 km		216
Severn	Dee	426	NNE of Melverley on Severn SJ 34 19	Dee at Coed-yr-Allt SJ 32 39	R	61	45	— 16 + 16	21	2·4	60	Bunter Sandstones 15 km. Upper Carboniferous 6 km	Aqueduct may be used in reverse direction	122
Severn	Dove	427	Severn at Sutton Wood SJ 70 01	Dove near Uttoxeter SK 12 31	R	35	69	+ 34	51	2·4	40	Enville Beds, Bunter and Keuper Sandstones 19 km. Keuper Marl 32 km		123
Severn	COVENTRY and Thames and Great Ouse via Cherwell	428	Upton on Severn SO 85 38	Bidford on Avon SP 11 52	R	11	35	+ 24	27	2·5	30	Keuper Marl and Lias Clay		229, 311
Ely Ouse	Grafham Water	429	Denver TF 59 00	Grafham Water TL 17 66	D/R/F	0	44* (See under Remarks)	+ 44	55	2·5	30	Oxford, Ampthill and Kimmeridge clays	*TWL of Grafham Water. Assumed that water supplied through tunnel would be detained temporarily in Grafham Water	143 to 147 inclusive

NOTES TO TABLES

(a) The grid references given are those of the south west corner of a 1 km grid square within which the point is situated.

(b) The elevation given for terminal points of aqueducts is normally ground level. Where aqueducts terminate at reservoirs the levels shown are the maximum and minimum levels of the water in storage as appropriate.

(c) The maximum static pressure head on an aqueduct is taken as the difference in levels either between the terminal points, or between any intermediate high point (summit) and the starting point. In most cases this static head difference is positive or, if negative, is insufficient to overcome friction head losses. In either case pumping would be required.

(d) Where pipes are duplicated they are assumed to be of the same diameter.

(e) Deficiency centres are shown in capital letters. Their location is notional (see Appendix D).

(f) An initial spare capacity is shown for existing aqueducts where their full potential capacity has not yet been taken up. Such capacities have been allowed for in allocating resources to future deficiencies.

(g) Typical depth of cover over tunnels is given in Table C.4 as either the depth below a general plateau level or the average depth below a more variable "saw-tooth" ground level, as appropriate.

(h) The diameter of standard 100 inch wedge block tunnels is shown as 2·5 m.

Appendix D

Schedule of Demand Districts and Deficiency Centres

Demand district	Statutory water undertakings in demand district	Grid ref and name of assumed deficiency centre delivery point	Elevation of delivery point feet OD	metres OD
NEWCASTLE	Newcastle and Gateshead W Co Tynemouth CBC	NZ 215 695 Gosforth	400	122
SUNDERLAND	Durham Co WB Hartlepools W Co Sunderland and S Shields W Co	NZ 320 500 New Lambton	400	122
TEESSIDE	Darlington CBC Tees Valley and Cleveland WB	NZ 378 203 Gatley Moor	300	91
NORTH AND EAST YORKS	Claro WB E Yorks (Wolds Area) WB Northallerton and the Dales WB Norton UDC Ryedale Jt WB Scarborough BC York WW Co	—	—	—
HULL	Kingston upon Hull CBC	SE 994 298 West Ella	250	76
HUMBERSIDE	NE Lincs WB N Lindsey WB	TA 012 073 Brigg	250	76
WEST RIDING NORTH	Bradford CBC Calderdale WB Craven WB Huddersfield CBC Leeds CBC Mid Calder WB Pontefract Goole and Selby WB Rombalds WB Wakefield and District WB	SE 240 286 Gildersome	550	168
SHEFFIELD/CHESTERFIELD	Barnsley CBC Central Notts WB Doncaster and Dist Jt WB N Derbyshire WB (excl part in Mersey and Weaver RA) Rawmarsh UDC Rotherham CBC Sheffield CBC Wortley RDC	SK 415 795 Eckington	500	152
CARLISLE/KENDAL	Carlisle Eden WB Furness WB Lakes and Lune WB Parish of Ulpha (no statutory undertaking)	—	—	—
WEST CUMBERLAND	S Cumberland WB W Cumberland WB	NY 002 222 Distington	350	107
FYLDE/PRESTON	Calder WB Fylde WB Lune Valley WB N Calder WB Preston and District WB	SD 614 377 Longridge	450	137
MANCHESTER	Bolton CBC Macclesfield Dist WB Makerfield WB Manchester CBC N Derby WB (part in Mersey and Weaver RA) Stockport and Dist WB W Pennine WB	SJ 792 955 Longford	360	110

Schedule of Demand Districts and Deficiency Centres continued

Demand district	Statutory water undertakings in demand district	Grid ref and name of assumed deficiency centre delivery point	Elevation of delivery point feet OD	metres OD
LIVERPOOL	Liverpool CBC St Helens CBC Warrington Runcorn and Dist WB W Lancs WB Widnes BC	SJ 473 937 Prescot	276	84
CHESTER/FLINT	Ceiriog RDC Central Flintshire WB Chester WW Co Maelor RDC Mid Cheshire WB Wirral WB Wrexham and E Denbighshire W Co Wrexham RDC	SJ 370 690 Chester	375	114
DENBIGH	W Denbighshire and W Flintshire WB	—	—	—
STOKE	Leek UDC Stafford BC Staffs Potteries WB	SJ 845 395 Trentham	700	213
NOTTINGHAM	Nottingham CBC S Derby WB	SK 455 375 Stanton	460	140
LEICESTER	Leicester CBC (excl part in Welland and Nene RA) NW Leics WB	SK 535 115 Cropston	470	143
CENTRAL LINCS	E Lincs WB Kesteven WB Lincoln and Dist WB	—	—	—
COVENTRY	Coventry CBC NE Warwick WB Rugby Jt WB S Warwicks WB	SP 425 785 Brinklow	310	94
CEGB 1		SJ 653 044 Ironbridge	135	41
CEGB 2		SO 840 470 Clifton	50	15
BIRMINGHAM	Birmingham CBC S Staffs WW Co Wolverhampton CBC	SO 920 918 Tipton	750	229
WORCESTER	E Worcs WWC NW Worcs WB SW Worcs WB	SO 890 600 Hindlip (NE Worcester)	375	114
GLOUCESTER	NW Glouc WB	SO 885 190 Churchdown	400	122
BRISTOL	Bath CBC Bristol WW Co (excl parts in Thames Conservancy and Somerset RA) N Wilts WB (excl parts in Avon and Dorset RA and Thames Conservancy) Swindon BC (part in Bristol Avon RA) W Wilts WB (part in Bristol Avon RA)	ST 615 775 Filton	400	122
CARDIFF	Cardiff CBC Gwent WB Industrial Estates Management Corp (Treforest) Mid-Glam WB Taf Fechan WB	ST 205 842 Lisvane	375	114

Demand district	Statutory water undertakings in demand district	Grid ref and name of assumed deficiency centre delivery point	Elevation of delivery point feet OD	metres OD
HEREFORD/BRECON	Herefordshire WB Radnorshire and N Breconshire WB SE Breconshire WB	—	—	—
DYFED	Cardigan WB Carmarthen BC and RDC Cwmamman UDC Llandeilo UDC and RDC Llandovery BC Llanelli and District WB Lougher Jt WB Pembroke WB W Glam WB	—	—	—
SALOP	E Shropshire WB Montgomeryshire WB W Shropshire WB	—	—	—
GWYNEDD	Anglesey CC Conway Valley WB Eryri WB Merioneth WB	—	—	—

NORTHAMPTON	Higher Ferrers and
	  Rushden WB
	Leicester CBC (part in
	  Welland and Nene RA)
	Mid Northants WB
		SP 827 712
		Hannington
			470	143

SOUTH LINCS	S Lincs WB	TF 106 015 Upton	175	53

TIDAL OUSE	NW Norfolk WB (excl
	  part in E Suffolk and
	  Norfolk RA)
	S Norfolk WB (excl part in
	  E Suffolk and
	  Norfolk RA)
	Wisbech and Dist WB
		TF 672 155
		Middleton
			130	40

CAMBRIDGE	Cambridge W Co
	Ely Mildenhall and
	  Newmarket WB
	W Suffolk WB (part in
	  Great Ouse RA)
		TL 493 548
		Cambridge
			200	61

NORTH ESSEX	Colchester and Dist WB Ipswich CBC Tendring Hundred WW Co W Suffolk WB (excl part in Great Ouse RA)	TM 020 330 Colchester	250	76
BEDS AND HUNTS	Bedfordshire WB Nene and Ouse WB	TL 041 392 Ampthill	415	126
BUCKS	Buckingham BC Bucks WB	SP 815 292 Mursley	500	152
UPPER LEE	Lee Valley W Co Luton W Co	TL 274 175 Welwyn	410	125
OXFORD	Cotswold WB Oxfordshire and Dist WB	SP 455 065 Farmoor	400	122

Schedule of Demand Districts and Deficiency Centres continued

Demand district	Statutory water undertakings in demand district	Grid ref and name of assumed deficiency centre delivery point	Elevation of delivery point feet OD	metres OD
COLNE	Chesham UDC Colne Valley W Co Rickmansworth and Uxbridge Valley W Co Watford BC	TQ 155 867 Harrow	380	116
LONDON	Croydon BC Epsom and Ewell BC Metropolitan WB Sutton and District W Co	TQ 314 828 Finsbury	250	76
SOUTH ESSEX	Essex W Co	TQ 634 914 Herongate	260	79

THAMES	Bristol WWC (part in
	  Thames Conservancy)
	E Surrey W Co (excl part
	  in Kent RA)
	Middle Thames WB
	Mid Southern W Co
	  (excl part in Sussex RA)
	N Wilts WB (parts in
	  Thames Conservancy)
	SW Suburban W Co
	S Wilts WB (parts in
	  Thames Conservancy)
	Southampton CBC (part
	  in Thames Conservancy)
	Swindon BC (excl parts in
	  Bristol Avon RA, Avon
	  and Dorset RA, Hants RA)
	Thames Valley WB (excl
	  part in Hants RA)
	W Surrey WB
	Woking and District W Co
		Variable—
		assumed 10 miles
		from respective
		Thames
		abstraction point
			400	122

KENT	SWU's in Kent RA (excl Metropolitan WB area)	—	—	—
SUSSEX	SWU's in Sussex RA area including Thames Conservancy areas of NW Sussex WB and Mid- Sussex W Co but excl E Surrey W Co and W Surrey WB	—	—	—
HAMPSHIRE	SWU's in Hampshire RA area	—	—	—
AVON AND DORSET	SWU's in Avon and Dorset RA area	—	—	—
ANGLIA	SWU's in E Suffolk and Norfolk RA area with all E Anglian W Co but excluding Ipswich CBC	—	—	—
SOMERSET	SWU's in Somerset RA area	—	—	—
DEVON	SWU's in Devon RA area	—	—	—
CORNWALL	SWU's in Cornwall RA area	—	—	—

Appendix E Cost assumptions

E.1 It is essential to have a consistent basis for comparing the costs of alternative programmes of resource development. This appendix sets out the main assumptions used in this study.

Component Costs

E.2 Table E.1 lists the basic rates and costs assumed for each of the main components of the capital and operating costs of alternative schemes. As cost differences between programmes may be small, it is important to ensure uniformity in selection and application of costs. Cost estimates for the various components should be prepared on the same basis so that the relationship between them is of the right order: one component must not assume disproportionate importance because it has been costed on a more generous basis or at a different rate. For example, the optimum development and allocation of a programme or the relative costs between one programme and another could be upset if the assumed relationship between, say, source costs and transmission costs was incorrect. The sensitivity of optimisation and of programme costs to the adopted component costs were examined by testing the effect of deliberately varying the estimates by large amounts so that the range of their validity could be verified.

Programme Costs

E.3 Development programmes were costed for the strategic source and aqueduct network for bulk delivery to deficiency centres as described in Chapter 8.

E.4 Programme costs comprise:

(i) capital and running costs of strategic sources;

(ii) capital and running costs of aqueducts forming part of the strategic source-demand system;

(iii) capital costs of water treatment works and service reservoirs and running costs of treatment works;

(iv) administration and maintenance.

E.5 Costs of programmes thus exclude all local sources and associated works and all costs of distribution from service reservoirs to consumers.

E.6 The programmes were devised to satisfy estimated deficiencies as they arise up to the year 2001 and thereafter to provide for the perpetual satisfaction of that level of demand. Sources were introduced as necessary to meet demands and their allocation was devised to give the least cost within the arrangement of sources and aqueduct links constituting a particular resource programme. The method used is described in Appendix F.

E.7 All the capital and running costs of programmes were calculated for each year from 1974 to 2001 and totalled for the period. The total costs and sub-divisions showing three categories of capital costs and three categories of running costs are set out in Table 16. These annual costs, together with replacement and running costs in perpetuity, were discounted back to 1974 to give a total "discounted cost" which takes into account the timing of necessary expenditure (see paragraphs 9–12 below). The currently recommended Treasury test discount rate of 10 per cent was used. Some of the costs are common to all programmes. These common elements are capital and running costs of standard two-stage treatment, service reservoirs and some sources and links; and administration costs. The remaining elements are those which cause the cost differences between programmes. The total and discounted cost of these variables are given in Table 16. The table also gives the differences in total and discounted costs of each of the other programmes from the least cost inland storage programme, A1.

Use of 1972 Prices

E.8 1972 prices have been used throughout, irrespective of the expected date of outlay. It is normal practice in making comparisons between alternatives to exclude the possible effects of future inflation on the level of costs. Inflation uniformly applied to all elements of the schemes would leave the alternatives in the same relative position. Different rates of inflation between, for example, the costs of sources, aqueducts and power could affect the relative costs. The sensitivity tests referred to in paragraph E.2 are also relevant to changes in costs arising in this way.

Discounted Costs

E.9 Discounted costs, or discounted cost differences between programmes, take into account the timing of investment required in the programme. They give a progressively lower value to expenditure incurred in later years by discounting these amounts to the base year chosen for the comparison. The differences in discounted costs represent the sum of money which if invested at that date would cover the additional cost of one programme over another over the period of development.

E.10 This basis of comparison is equivalent to assuming that any money which is not expended at the outset (the base year) is invested instead and earns interest until it is needed for the next stage of the programme. A corollary of this concept is that money spent in the future rather than now will save interest on borrowing over the intervening years.

Choice of Date for Discounting

E.11 The costs of the alternative programmes of source development shown in Table 16 have been discounted to 1974, which is the date from which costs are assumed to be incurred. The significance of 1974 is that the first decisions on the options presented in this report will need to be taken by then. This applies not only to the sources recommended for development to meet needs arising by 1981, but also by implication to some sources needed after that date. In particular an early decision is essential on the choice between integrated and regionally-based strategies. Other decisions for implementation after 1981, such as the choice between transfers from the Severn to the Thames and further storage in the Thames catchment, will have to be made in 1974 or soon thereafter.

E.12 Other options in the programmes will not need to be exercised for a number of years, although they will in some cases be influenced by decisions taken earlier. These consequential choices will be made in the light of relative costs and other considerations at the time of decision. In the meantime discounting the costs of complete programmes to 1974 gives an indication at this stage of the comparative cost of the options.

Discount Rate

E.13 Variations in the discounting rate can influence the cost comparison between the alternative programmes. A low discount rate (the total undiscounted costs are equivalent to a zero discount rate) tends to favour large schemes involving high expenditure in early years and with a relatively low initial utilisation of the output. Conversely a high discount rate favours development of large schemes in stages, or of a larger number of smaller schemes brought into service as demands rise even though the total cost may be greater than that of an alternative large scheme. Such a course delays capital investment and involves a higher utilisation of the capacity of the installations. Low discount rates also favour schemes with higher initial capital expenditure if this is coupled with lower running costs later; the opposite is true of high rates. In order to test the validity of programme comparisons with different discount rates, discounted costs were determined for certain programmes using discount rates of 6, 8 and 12 per cent as well as the rate of 10 per cent adopted for general comparison.

Discounted Unit Cost of Sources

E.14   One method of calculating unit cost is to divide the total annual costs (loan charges, plus operating costs at full yield) by the annual output of the source at full capacity. This gives the conventional "Unit Cost". It is realistic only if the capacity is fully utilised from the outset, which is seldom the case, especially with large sources. Conventional unit costs tend therefore to be misleadingly low especially where the available yield is not taken up for many years.

E.15   The effect of timing of expenditure on the capital and running costs of a source, and the timing of utilisation of its output, can be taken into account by determining the Discounted Unit Cost (DUC).

E.16   The DUC is derived by discounting to a selected base year (conveniently the date of initial expenditure) the capital and operating costs incurred to keep the source in operation in perpetuity. This is then divided by a measure of the quantity of water to be provided by the source, obtained by discounting at the same rate and to the same base year as the expenditure, the quantities to be supplied year by year in perpetuity. The resulting DUC represents, in discounted terms, the cost at which water could be sold from the source, considered in isolation, so as just to break even at the time horizon. It permits economic comparison of schemes of different scale which would reach full use at different dates and after different periods.

E.17   Source Tables A.1 to A.6, Appendix A, include, in addition to capital costs and annual power costs, DUCs for four different rates of take-up of yield; namely, instantaneous take-up (corresponding substantially to conventional unit cost), and at 100, 50 and 25 thousand cu.m.d. per annum. For large sources unit values rise rapidly as the rate of take-up of yield falls. The values given take account of capital cost, staging where appropriate, replacements to perpetuity and power costs to perpetuity. Replacement periods are assumed as follows:—

Dams, tunnels and heavy concrete works	Over 60 years
Pipes 900 mm diameter and over, river intakes, reinforced concrete reservoirs	40 years
Pipes under 900 mm diameter, pumphouses, treatment plant	30 years
Pumps and machinery	15 years

1972 Cost Schedule

E.18   The 1967 rates adopted for our studies of the North and of Wales and the Midlands were used as the basis for arriving at the 1972 costs set out in the accompanying schedule. The 1967 rates were updated in the light of periodically published statistics of costs of new works in the construction and building industry, and of recent tenders and consulting engineers' estimates for large works. As the works costed comprise the larger strategic sources and bulk transmission links, estimates for larger works were regarded as the most relevant. The advice and data provided by the Water Research Association were used for water treatment costs and the U.K. Atomic Energy Authority gave guidance in selecting appropriate costs for desalination of seawater.

E.19   This updating resulted in an appreciable increase in the costs of transmission links, treatment works and treatment operation, in each case greater than the general rate of inflation over the five years. Source costs on the other hand increased over the period by less than the general rate of inflation. This lower rate of increase was partly due to a reduction in real costs arising from improved construction techniques, but also to the fact that estimates for source costs in the 1967 schedule were more generous than those for most other items.

Source Costs

E.20   Following recommendations in our reports on the South-East, the North and Wales and the Midlands, consulting engineers have carried out feasibility studies of many of the sources included in the present study. Individual estimates are now available for these. The basis for costing has varied considerably, as have the dates to which the estimates apply. The need was therefore to adjust these estimates for sources for the sake of consistency and to update them to 1972 prices, rather than to build up costs from general basic rates. This is reflected in the rates and cost schedule. Where no detailed studies have yet been made, desk study estimates or regional study preliminary estimates have been similarly updated.

Transmission Link Costs

E.21   Transmission link costs include the cost of aqueducts and river intakes, raw water storage, pumphouses and pumps, and the cost of power for pumping where applicable. Few of the potential transmission links have so far been fully investigated, but for comparative purposes and because link optimisation was a feature of the studies, the basic rates in the schedule were generally adopted. The cost optimisation of pipeline links has sought to minimise the combined capital and pumping costs, taking into account such factors as:

(i)   variations in flow over the years according to the changing source-demand pattern;

(ii)   frequency of use of pipelines between rivers and between rivers and storage which are used intermittently (load factor);

(iii)   the relationship between maximum filling rate and yield of pump filled sources (raw water pump factor);

(iv)   staging (duplication) of pipelines;

(v)   acceptable maximum velocities of flow in pipelines.

E.22   Certain tunnel links were investigated in more detail and individual estimates made. These were taken into account not only for those particular routes, but in establishing the general rates for application to other routes which have not so far been investigated and costed individually.

Common Cost Elements

E.23   To complete the estimate of cost of works from source to terminal storage, the following were included:

(i)   capital costs of treatment works and service reservoirs;

(ii)   running costs of treatment works and cost of administration, including day to day running and maintenance of the works taken as pro rata to the quantities of water supplied.

E.24   Here too representative rates are considered appropriate and adequate for present purposes. In practice the departure from any of these assumed rates would not have a significant differential effect on programme costs and would not therefore invalidate comparisons between alternatives.

Table E.1
Schedule of 1972 Rates and Costs

Item	Description	Imperial		Metric (See Note 1)		Remarks
		Unit	Rate or cost	Unit	Rate or cost	
	A—Capital costs					
1	Dams, including spillways, outlet and ancillary works	item	Regional study estimate +5% per annum from date of estimate updating to 1972 *or* Consulting engineers' estimate +5% per annum updating to 1972	item	As in previous column	Original estimates, prior to updating to 1972 prices, are adjusted to include all items listed in Note 2. Construction periods (see Note 3) are assumed to be as follows:— Capital cost up to £1·25M — 1 year; £1·25M to £6·25M — 2 years; £6·25M to £12·5M — 3 years; Exceeding £12·5M — 4 years
2	Estuarial embankments and associated heavy civil engineering works	item	Consulting engineers' feasibility study estimate +5% per annum updating to 1972 *or* Consulting engineers' desk study estimate +10% per annum updating to 1972	item	As in previous column	Construction periods are assumed to be as estimated by the consulting engineers
3	Light civil engineering works associated with estuarial storage	item	Consulting engineers' estimate +8% per annum updating to 1972	item	As in previous column	
4	River intakes	mgd	£1 000	thousand cu.m.d	£220	
5	Raw water storage	mgd	£32 000	thousand cu.m.d	£7 000	7 days storage assumed
6	Pump houses	mgd	£4 000	thousand cu.m.d	£880	
7	Pipelines					Construction period for pipelaying contracts is assumed to be 1½ years
	18 in dia (450 mm)	mile	£40 000	km	£24 000	
	36 in dia (900 mm)	mile	£100 000	km	£61 000	Intermediate diameters linearly interpolated
	72 in dia (1800 mm)	mile	£280 000	km	£170 000	
8	Tunnels in rock					Construction periods are assumed to be as follows:— Length in miles between portals / Construction period in years: Less than 4 — 2; 4 to 7 — 3; 7 to 9 — 4
	6·5 ft dia (2·0 m)	mile	£550 000	km	£343 000	
	8 ft dia (2·4 m)	mile	£610 000	km	£376 000	
	12 ft dia (3·7 m)	mile	£890 000	km	£559 000	
9	Tunnels in clay, 100 in dia (2540 mm)	mile	£325 000	km	£200 000	Construction period is assumed to be normally 2 years
10	Treatment works, inclusive of buildings and plant for standard two-stage treatment (filtration and sedimentation)	mgd through-put	£65 000	thousand cu.m.d through-put	£14 300	
11	Terminal storage in service reservoirs	mgd through-put	£45 500	thousand cu.m.d through-put	£10 000	
12	Pumps and associated equipment including standby plant	WHP	£130	Output kW	£175	
13	Groundwater sources		Various		Various	See Appendix A, Table A.5 for specific schemes, including artificial recharge projects
	B—Running costs					
14	Power for high lift pumps and groundwater pumping	1000 gallons per 100 ft lift	0·333p (equivalent to £12·17 per mgd per foot total head per annum at 100% load factor)	cu.m per 100 m lift	0·24p	Unit costs are based on a power charge of 0·625p/kWh. An overall efficiency of 70% for motor and pump has been assumed
15	Two-stage treatment: power, labour and chemicals	1000 gallons	2·00p (equivalent to £7300 mgd per annum)	cu.m	0·44p	
16	Additional treatment		Varies		Varies	Costs vary according to specific requirements
17	Administration and overheads	1000 gallons	1·25p	cu.m	0·275p	

Notes: 1 Imperial units were used for costing development programmes. Costs for metric sizes are rounded equivalents of those for imperial sizes.
2 Mid-1972 rates and prices are used and include engineering design and supervision, land acquisition, ancillary works such as road diversions, engineering contingencies, but exclude interest on capital during construction.
3 In calculating discounted costs of development programmes and in estimating discounted unit costs of water at the various sources listed in Appendix A, construction periods are assumed as indicated in the schedule to establish dates from which expenditure is discounted. In this way interest during construction is taken into account as equivalent to the discount rate, i.e. 10 per cent per annum. Where no construction period is indicated costs are discounted from the year of completion.

Appendix F The analysis of water resource systems

Introduction

F.1   The purpose of this Appendix is to outline the application of systems analysis to water resource planning and to describe how it has been used to allocate sources to demands and to compare the costs of programmes of resource development included in our report. This Appendix is concerned only with the planning stage of the development of a water resource system; it is not concerned with design and operation.

A Water Resource System

F.2   A water resource system consists of physical components such as sources, aqueducts and treatment plants and its use is constrained by non-physical aspects such as flood control, water quality standards, statutory restrictions and licensing of water abstraction from rivers and lakes. The demands on the system include industrial and domestic water supply, satisfaction of requirements for minimum river flows, and largely unquantifiable considerations relating to planning, amenity, land use, conservation and sociology.

F.3   All this represents the interference of man with the hydrological cycle in an attempt to balance supply and demand; a relatively simple task if demands are individual and cumulative. Demands, however, are generally interactive and in varying degree conflicting. Examples of this are:

  (i)   one deficiency centre competing against another for the yield of a source;

  (ii) re-use along the river system;

  (iii) demands for abstraction competing with the need for water in the river;

  (iv) costs competing with amenity considerations.

Systems Analysis

F.4   During the last 10 years systems analysis with mathematical models has been used increasingly in planning, designing and operating systems of water resources. This technique can rationalise the complex problems of many inter-related causes and effects such as occur in sophisticated water resource developments. In principle there is nothing new in this. It consists of stating what is expected of a system, identifying ways of achieving it, and then assessing the performance and cost of the alternatives. What are new (in practice if not in concept) are the techniques of computation used for optimisation and simulation, made feasible by the use of electronic computers for handling the large volume of data and computations involved.

F.5   There are two main principles:

  (i)   it is better to solve a problem by breaking it down into a large number of simple units rather than a small number of complex units;

  (ii) a system changes with time and it is assumed that its state in one time period is related to its state in a previous time period.

Analytical Models

F.6   The most important object of systems analysis as we use it in water resource planning is to make the optimum choice from amongst a range of options. This process of optimisation relies on mathematical theory related to the maximisation and minimisation of functions, known collectively as the mathematics of extrema. This theory is partly based on calculus, but this by itself can only be used in simple cases where there are no restrictions imposed by real life situations. For the analysis of complex systems iterative techniques can be used. These involve the optimising of an objective (for instance the minimising of a cost function) within the constraints expressed by a set of mathematical equations which define the system and its requirements.

Simulation Models

F.7   Difficulties in the analysis of complex systems are:

  (i)   systems may be impossible or extremely costly to observe;

  (ii) systems may not lend themselves to a mathematical description from which analytical solutions can be obtained;

  (iii) even if this is possible the resulting equation may not be of use for predicting future conditions;

  (iv) the resulting equation may be either too complex to analyse, too costly to compute or require unavailable data.

F.8   These difficulties can be overcome to a certain extent by using simulation models. These abstract those features of the system which affect decisions on its planning, design and operation. If the aim of the study is to find optimum values, simulation is used in a trial and error fashion. The user asks questions by specifying certain courses of action; the simulation provides answers in the form of the likely consequences of these actions. It is, however, the responsibility of the user to ask the right questions.

F.9   An example of a very simple model is an instruction—"if the flow rate in a river is greater than 10 pump the surplus water into a reservoir, keeping a record of the total pumped". Therefore with a flow sequence of 11, 12, 13, 14, 15, 10, 8 the total amount pumped would be 15. The value "greater than 10" in the instruction is the control rule which can be varied. If, on running the sequence through the model again, the control rule was changed to a value of 8 the total quantity pumped would be 27.

F.10   This approach is simple. It follows the first principle of systems analysis (paragraph F.5), the use of simple components. However, the computational load quickly escalates; if, for example, the model is used for 100 years of daily flows about 36,500 individual calculations would be made. It must then be extended to include further instructions: for example, "The reservoir is full today, do not pump" and "The full surplus cannot be pumped today because the capacity of the pumps is only 5". This process can continue until the number of options built into the model is very large. In this way simulation models are built; simple components join together to make a complex model.

Computation for Systems Analysis

F.11   There are four principal steps in the use of systems analysis if a computer is used:

  (i)   formulating a mathematical model which orders the physical elements and the non-physical constraints in their correct cause and effect relationship;

  (ii) collating data as input to the model;

  (iii) writing a computer program to represent the model;

  (iv) using the computer program as an experimental medium to study the system the program represents.

The Models Used in the Study

F.12   The objective of the study undertaken for our report was to identify and select co-ordinated strategies of resource development to meet increasing demands for water in England and Wales for the rest of the century. Initially a vast number of options was available from different permutations and combinations of sources. These had to be reduced first to a small number of different strategies and then to the best variations or programmes within each strategy. The identification of feasible programmes from which a choice could be made was aided by systems analysis, but subjective judgement also played a part.

F.13   Two complementary models were devised. The first was an analytical model which indicated the least discounted cost programme of resource development within a selected broad strategy, e.g. Strategy B, Estuary Storage Sources. The second was a model which simulated the construction and operation of one resource development programme at a time to obtain detailed analyses of costs. The programmes selected for this further analysis were based on the results of the first model. The models were designed to incorporate the results of more detailed studies and to take account of decisions already made on the promotion of certain schemes.

F.14   The first step in the use of each of the models was identical. It was to collect and collate the data in terms suitable for use in the study forming the basis of the report. The activities within this step may be summarised as follows:

(i)   Public water supply undertakings were grouped together into demand districts taking into account existing and proposed supply arrangements.

(ii)   Current and future demands of the water undertakings and net direct future demands by industry and agriculture were assessed for each district, taking into account the re-use of effluents to meet certain of these increasing demands—especially direct industrial demands.

(iii)   The yields of existing and authorised sources were also assessed.

(iv)   For each district the differences between the estimated future net demands and the yields of existing and authorised sources able to meet them were calculated to arrive at the total future deficiencies in specific years (1981 and 2001).

(v)   Sixteen of the demand districts where the estimated deficiencies could best be met by local sources isolated from an integrated resources system, were then classified as self-sufficient.

(vi)   The remaining 36 demand districts, were treated as having a "strategic deficiency" to be met from integrated source development. This was incorporated in the models for the analysis. To enable representative costs for supply of water to the districts to be obtained each of the districts was represented, both geographically and topographically, by a notional deficiency centre.

(vii)   Strategic sources were identified to meet these resulting deficiencies.

(viii)   Aqueduct routes were selected to provide links between sources and deficiency centres. The choice between tunnels or pipelines and the required size was determined by the flow patterns in a particular development programme.

(ix)   Costs were estimated using the figures set out in Appendix E, Table E.1. They are mostly costs prevailing in mid-1972, but where data on specific sources or aqueducts were available from the reports of undertakings or consultants, they were used after adjustment to a common basis related to 1972.

Analytical Model for Optimisation of Resource System Costs
F.15   The cost data showed, as expected, economies of scale. However the curves representing these costs had to be approximated in linear form so that they could be used in the model. The costs and yields of the sources, and the length and pumping heads of the links were incorporated into the model as single discrete values.

F.16   The optimising technique used in this model is integer programming, an extension of linear programming. The formulation of the resource allocation problem in an integer programming model entails the description of the physical system (in this case a network of deficiency centres, aqueducts and sources) and its requirements in terms of linear equations called constraints. The model was required to minimise, within these constraints, the total of discounted capital and running costs to perpetuity.

F.17   The technique can take into account the fact that many decision variables are of the "yes or no" type. An example of such a decision is whether or not a reservoir should be built within a particular time period, for which a fractional value would have no meaning.

F.18   The description of a potential water resources system for England and Wales has required the use of several thousand variables and constraints. The efficient solution of problems of this magnitude requires the use of sophisticated integer programming packages available at consultancy bureaux. One such program system was found to be suitable and was used for our study. In order to use this standard package, a program was written to formulate the model of the water resource system and manipulate the standard optimising system. This method first produces an approximate solution; second, using a refined search technique (known as the "branch-and-bound" technique), a feasible solution, and finally the best feasible solution.

F.19   For some of the strategies outlined in Chapter 8 the model was used to determine the optimal solution. For each of four time periods the model indicates which links and sources are required in the given time periods. It also indicates the flows in the system and the programme with the least total discounted cost for the particular set of source, link and demand assumptions comprising a strategy. Due to the complex nature of the model the output cannot be detailed in cost terms.

Simulation Model for Resource Allocation and Costing
F.20   The analysis of the basic data for use in this model is similar to that for the analytical model except that the costs of the link components do not have to be linear, but can be expressed in a continuous form. The data are kept on computer files which are used by the computer programs when required.

F.21   The model is based on a suite of computer programs written by our staff which accept the basic data representing the physical network and carry out a specified analysis. Five stages can be identified in the analysis of a resource development programme.

(i)   The order of introduction of the sources is specified.

(ii)   For each year within the time scale of the analysis the model allocates water from the sources available to the deficiency centres in a predetermined sequence which is based on the least cost of supplying each centre from each source.

(iii)   Using these allocation data and basic hydrological data the patterns of the maximum flows likely to result and the average flows are computed.

(iv)   Each of the pipeline links is then analysed to determine the optimal plan for the staging and sizing of pipe and pump installations.

(v)   The final stage determines the cost and the present value of implementing the investment and operating decisions.

F.22   The costs of implementing a wide range of resource development programmes were simulated by the model. A selection of programmes and cost data computed are shown in Table 16.

Appendix G Groundwater for river regulation and conjunctive use with surface water

Introduction

G.1   Large volumes of water are stored in aquifers. Conventional methods of using groundwater generally take little account of the availability of this natural storage capacity. As the demand for water increases so will the need to exploit such natural resources more effectively without detriment to the environment. This can be done either by using groundwater for river regulation or by conjunctive use of separate surface and groundwater sources. These two approaches are outlined below.

River Regulation by Groundwater

G.2   The storage capacity of aquifers can be used to regulate rivers by pumping groundwater into them to supplement low flows. This is similar to making releases from surface storage for the same purpose. There are two principal methods of doing this:

   (i)   Pump continuously from wells directly into supply and maintain residual river flows, which are reduced by this pumping, by intermittently discharging groundwater into the rivers.

   (ii) Pump from wells into rivers to maintain a prescribed flow, part of which is abstracted lower down the river, either through a river intake, or, if geological conditions are suitable by abstraction from wells adjacent to the river, thereby inducing recharge from the river.

G.3   The feasibility of river regulation by pumping groundwater from the Chalk has been investigated by the Thames Conservancy and the Great Ouse River Authority. Both authorities are now designing schemes, which together will produce 785 thousand cu.m.d. by the end of the century. Approval has been given to the first stage of the Thames groundwater scheme. Drilling has commenced and it is expected that all stages of the scheme will be completed by the early 1980s.

G.4   The Severn and Yorkshire River Authorities are examining the scope for regulating the Severn and the Yorkshire Ouse respectively by pumping from the Triassic sandstones.

Conjunctive Use of Groundwater and Surface Water Without River Regulation

G.5   This is intermittent use of groundwater and surface water, generally from hydrologically separate sources. Groundwater is pumped directly to supply at times when abstraction from surface sources is limited by low flows. In this case, river flows are not augmented by groundwater, but the balancing use of groundwater instead of the river for direct supply reduces the depletion of surface resources during dry periods.

G.6   In the Fylde area of Lancashire the Triassic sandstones are being developed in conjunction with abstraction from the Lune and from surface storage in reservoirs in the Pennines to yield 150 thousand cu.m.d. as a first stage. It may also be possible to develop the Triassic sandstones of the Midlands in conjunction with the rivers of the Peak District of Derbyshire.

Yields and Inter-Relation between Groundwater and River Flows

G.7   Groundwater gives a higher overall yield if pumped intermittently to regulate river flows or if used in conjunction with surface sources than if pumped continuously direct to supply. There are two reasons for this. First, an aquifer can yield at a higher rate when drawn on over shorter periods. Second, such controlled use allows comparatively heavy depletion of the aquifer in dry periods which is replenished during periods of natural recharge. Where groundwater is used for river regulation flows are augmented by pumping even though the water level in the aquifer is drawn down so that it contributes less naturally to river flows.

G.8   In most schemes combining groundwater with river abstraction the groundwater is pumped only during periods of low flow, which normally occur in the summer. Even where the aquifer is used all the year round maximum pumping is in the summer. As a consequence of pumping, the water table is lowered below its natural level and the contribution from the aquifer to river flows is reduced in the following winter. This is because natural recharge, that is infiltration from rainfall, replenishes the depleted aquifer storage instead of contributing directly to river flows. There is, therefore, a net gain in flow during the summer and a net reduction in winter.

G.9   The gain in river flow will often be less than the quantity of water pumped because pumping from wells intercepts groundwater which would otherwise have been discharged naturally into the river. If pumping lowers groundwater levels below river level, water may leak or recirculate from the river back into the aquifer. It is necessary to consider these possibilities when selecting sites for abstraction wells.

G.10   There is a time lag between pumping water from a well and the effect on springs or other points of natural discharge to the river system. This is because of the slow movement of water through an aquifer and the buffering effect of the large volume of groundwater in storage. To take advantage of this, wells should be sited away from rivers, the distance depending upon the permeability and storage characteristics of the aquifer. In some situations, however, where the river bed is relatively impermeable and any recirculation would be small, there are distinct advantages in siting wells close to the river and concentrating the pumping within a limited area. This minimises transmission costs and reduces the area affected by the pumping.

G.11   The development of groundwater is ultimately limited by the long-term average infiltration, unless over development is accepted or artificial recharge is practised. During dry periods when river flows need augmenting, groundwater may be abstracted at a rate considerably in excess of the average infiltration to the aquifer, provided this is offset by a lower rate of abstraction at other times—when indeed the abstraction for river augmentation can be reduced to nil. Pumping disturbs the natural equilibrium in the hydrological system. The length of time required to establish a new equilibrium depends upon the pumping programme, the properties of the aquifer and the location of the wells in relation to the river. In some cases a new equilibrium may take many years to establish.

G.12   The yield of a groundwater regulation scheme depends upon the amount of water from storage that can be used during the critical design drought and the extent to which using this water lowers groundwater levels in relation to the thickness of the aquifer. This in turn depends upon the storage coefficient[1] of the aquifer, which is about 20 per cent for river gravels, 10 per cent for sandstones, such as the Triassic sandstones, but only about 2 per cent for the Chalk. Thus abstracting groundwater from storage equivalent in amount to an average annual infiltration of 300 mm represents a change in groundwater level of 3 m in sandstone and one of 15 m in Chalk. A decline in groundwater levels of 3 m in the Triassic sandstones is small in relation to the average thickness of this aquifer, but a decline of 15 m in the Chalk could be significant; because although the Chalk has a thickness

---

1 The quantity of water that can be obtained from a unit volume of rock is called the storage coefficient.

of up to 300 m, the fissured thickness, through which most of the water that can be extracted flows, is frequently less, in some areas only of the order of 50 to 60 m.

G.13   Because the storage coefficient is so important, careful investigation of aquifer properties is required before siting wells in a confined aquifer (that is where impermeable strata overlie the aquifer) if they are to be used for river regulation. In a confined aquifer water is held under pressure and the storage coefficient is of the order of 0·01 per cent. The consequences of groundwater abstraction are transmitted quickly through the aquifer to the outcrop areas and may affect river flows thereby reducing the net gain from pumping to uneconomic levels after a relatively short period of time.

G.14   In many cases it will be necessary to site wells some distance from rivers because of the risks of groundwater interception and re-circulation described in para G.9. In such areas the aquifer is likely to be less permeable (particularly if the Chalk is the aquifer involved) and more wells will be required to provide a given yield.

Conclusion

G.15   Groundwater pumped direct to supply is generally relatively cheap, due to low treatment costs, but it does lead to depletion of dependent river flows, particularly during the summer. When ground-water is used to regulate rivers the cost of treating water taken from the river increases, but this increase in cost is more than offset by the gain to yield and by benefits to amenity and fisheries which result from the augmentation of river flows in dry weather. Such schemes are therefore generally to be preferred to continuous direct pumping from an aquifer.

Appendix H Artificial recharge

Introduction

H.1   Artificial recharge would normally be considered as the third and last stage of groundwater development after direct abstraction from an aquifer and combined use of groundwater and surface water. In both cases yields are limited by the amount of natural recharge of the aquifer from rainfall. Yields may then be augmented by recharging the aquifer artifically with surplus surface water. Thus artificial recharge increases the level of development of a complete river catchment.

H.2   Artificial recharge can also be used in certain circumstances to purify polluted surface water. It is used, too, to prevent saline intrusion of aquifers.

H.3   Where land is available on an aquifer exposed at the surface, open lagoons or basins can be used to recharge the aquifer. It is then possible both to augment storage and to improve quality during recharge. Where, however, the aquifer is overlain by impervious strata or where land is not available for large scale recharge lagoons, wells can be used as an alternative. Recharge through wells is used for refilling aquifer storage rather than for improving the quality of the water recharged, and it normally requires good quality water.

H.4   In collaboration with several river authorities and the Metropolitan Water Board we are carrying out comprehensive studies of the technique of artificial recharge. Laboratory research is in hand at the Water Research Association and some field experiments have been carried out notably by the Metropolitan Water Board who began work on artificial recharge in the Lee Valley about 20 years ago.

London Basin Recharge Experiments

H.5   We have undertaken a comprehensive assessment of the potential for artificial recharge in the London Basin and have published a report, "Artificial Recharge of the London Basin I—Hydrogeology" (WRB 1972). Hydrogeological conditions are particularly favourable for artificial recharge in the Lee valley and the Leyton—Dagenham area. Available underground storage in the Lee valley amounts to almost 205 million cu.m. and in the Leyton—Dagenham area 115 million cu.m. Recharge of the Chalk at outcrop should also be feasible in the Wandle and Ravensbourne catchments where storage of 36 million cu.m. could be created by a general lowering of groundwater levels.

H.6   Steady state and non-steady state electrical analogue studies have been carried out. The results are reported in "Artificial Recharge of the London Basin II—Electrical Analogue Model Studies" (WRB 1973). This modelling work has helped to confirm the conclusions of the hydrogeological studies. It has also identified areas where there are anomalies in the observed data. Problems of saline intrusion from the Thames estuary have been investigated and potential solutions by well recharge have been studied.

H.7   For each of the areas identified in the hydrogeological report economic and feasibility studies have been carried out. Digital modelling techniques were used to determine the optimum spacing of recharge wells under various recharge and abstraction regimes. The relationship between groundwater storage developed by artificial recharge and different levels of surface water storage in the Thames basin has been studied in order to measure the increased yield from artificial recharge. This work will be reported in "Artificial Recharge of the London Basin III—Feasibility and Costs" to be published shortly.

H.8   In order to substantiate the theoretical studies, two field recharge experiments are being carried out in the middle Lee valley. At one site two recharge wells 600 mm in diameter have been constructed side by side. One well is arranged to recharge the Thanet Sands only, and the other only the Chalk. Mains water has been recharged at up to 5 thousand cu.m.d. and the quantitative and qualitative effects have been observed in seven observation wells. Similarly, mains water has been recharged at an existing Metropolitan Water Board site where the usefulness of adits has been studied. This experimental work will be fully reported in "Artificial Recharge of the London Basin IV—Field Studies" to be published in 1974.

H.9   The Lee Conservancy Catchment Board are investigating a prototype scheme, using existing and new wells in the Lee valley, to yield about 90 thousand cu.m.d.

H.10   In the London Basin there is ample storage available underground because the aquifer has been greatly overdeveloped. Phased use of this storage, in conjunction with the Thames and existing surface storage, may ultimately achieve an estimated additional yield of up to 400 thousand cu.m.d. from the Thames system.

Lagoon Recharge for Quality Improvement

H.11   Lagoon recharge experiments were carried out near Mansfield in Nottinghamshire during 1970 and 1971 with the help of the Trent River Authority. The object was to assess recharge rates and the degree of quality improvement attained when recharging a polluted river water similar in quality to the Trent at Nottingham. A basin 30 m square and 10 m deep was recharged at rates up to 4·5 thousand cu.m.d. The conclusions may be summarised as follows:

   (i)   Infiltration rates averaging up to 0·35 metres per day are feasible and, on the basis that the total land required is four times the area of water being recharged at any time, recharge approaching 90 thousand cu.m.d. per square kilometre can be achieved.

   (ii) Water quality was greatly improved. Suspended matter including pathogenic bacteria and viruses was removed and organic compounds were greatly reduced by adsorption and bio-degradation. Ammonia was completely oxidised and phosphate largely removed, although hardness and alkalinity increased. Heavy metals, at low levels throughout, were barely affected. The removal of organic pollutants over a long period was demonstrated by tests carried out at sewage treatment works where effluent has been discharged over the ground for up to 80 years.

Well Recharge for Storage Development—Trent Area

H.12   In the Clipstone Forest well recharge scheme near Mansfield, potable water has been recharged at rates up to 3·5 thousand cu.m.d. into a well 1 m in diameter and 63 m deep where the natural groundwater level is approximately 35 m below surface. The well is equipped with a stainless steel screen, gravel pack and permanent pump. These tests were carried out between June 1971 and September 1972 after a detailed hydrogeological investigation including the construction of eleven observation holes.

Triassic Sandstones in Nottinghamshire

H.13   There are two possible ways of using the Triassic Sandstones in Nottinghamshire. The first is recharge by lagoons for improving the quality of water abstracted from the Trent downstream of Nottingham. Dry weather flows in the Trent are adequate to allow abstractions exceeding 1 million cu.m.d., without need for supporting storage, but the quality is relatively poor. The improvement brought about by artificial recharge and percolation through the sandstones would be invaluable and this is likely to be a necessary stage in treating Trent water if it is to be used for potable supplies in the future.

H.14 The second proposal is to recharge the Triassic sandstones through boreholes with water taken from the relatively clean Derbyshire Derwent, a tributary of the Trent. The aquifer storage would be used in conjunction with abstraction from the river to augment supplies in periods of low flow. The quantity abstracted from the aquifer would be increased from the present amount which just about fully exploits the resources of natural recharge. Quality improvement in this case would be marginal and incidental.

Potential for Artificial Recharge

H.15 Eight possible schemes of development of artificial recharge are set out in Table H.1, including the three discussed in the preceding paragraphs. The other five are still at an early stage of consideration.

H.16 The work already done by us and by other organisations on research, desk studies and pilot schemes has shown that the artificial recharge of some of the country's aquifers is feasible and that the estimated costs of water supplied in this way are comparable with costs of supplies from other sources more commonly used at present. A major advantage of developing groundwater storage is that it can be done in stages; so can artificial recharge. Small schemes of basin or well recharge can be designed and implemented now to meet local demands and to serve as prototypes for further development later.

H.17 The only artificial recharge scheme included as a strategic source in our proposals for England and Wales is in the London Basin where the potential is greatest and where investigations into the feasibility are in a more advanced state than elsewhere. Recharge of the London Basin is included as a potential source for selection as and when it has been proved on an adequate scale. For this reason it is only included in programmes of source development towards the end of the century, but this may prove an unduly conservative assessment; continuing investigations may establish a case for its earlier development.

H.18 Most of the other aquifers in England and Wales not listed in the table are either still underdeveloped or are remote from a suitable source of recharge water. In most cases the hydrogeology requires further investigation before reliable estimates can be made of the possibilities for artificial recharge. Other work needed before this potential can be exploited includes economic and engineering feasibility assessments and field experiments to provide data for desk analyses. These aquifers are only likely, therefore, to be developed and to contribute to the demand for water in the longer term. None the less total yields of the order of 3·2 million cu.m.d. might ultimately be realised. The extent to which artificial recharge will play a part in water resource development in England and Wales depends on the degree of success achieved as schemes are implemented in stages in various localities under carefully designed conditions.

Artificial Recharge Overseas

H.19 Lagoon recharge is used in Germany to improve the quality of the water abstracted from the Ruhr and from other tributaries of the Rhine. Similarly, in Holland the dune sands are recharged with water from the Rhine to prevent intrusion of seawater into the aquifer and to augment natural groundwater for public supply. Similar methods are used in Scandinavia, France, Czechoslovakia, Hungary and the USA. Well recharge into sandstones and fissured limestone is practised in Israel. On Long Island, New York, recharge of sewage effluent near to the coast prevents saline intrusion and thus protects the quality of groundwater further inland. None of these cases is, however, similar in all respects to the circumstances and requirements in this country.

Table H.1
Potential Artificial Recharge Schemes in England and Wales

Location	Geology	Recharge by basins (B) or wells (W)	Description of scheme	Estimated maximum practicable yield thousand cu.m.d	Approximate capital cost £ million	Remarks
Nottinghamshire Nottingham/Mansfield/ Worksop area	Triassic sandstones at outcrop	B	Purification of Trent water by pre-treatment followed by percolation through and temporary storage in Triassic sandstones	1400	50	Part of this source is included in the costed programmes—see Appendix A, Table A.6
Nottinghamshire Nottingham/Mansfield area	Triassic sandstones at outcrop	W	Artificial recharge of aquifer storage in the middle Trent from the Derwent to augment yield of Conjunctive Use Scheme	360	25	This scheme could be a follow-up development of the middle Trent Conjunctive Use Scheme (natural recharge) —see Appendix A, Table A.6
London Basin	Confined Chalk and Lower London Tertiary sands	W	Artificial recharge of depleted aquifer storage from the Thames to augment yield of combined aquifer/surface storage/river system	400	20	Part of this source is included in the costed programmes—see Appendix A, Table A.5
Yorkshire Vale of York	Triassic sandstones covered with permeable drift	W or possibly B	Artificial recharge of aquifer storage from the Ure and Swale to augment yield of natural recharge groundwater regulation scheme for Ouse	360	10	This scheme could follow development of the Vale of York groundwater scheme (natural recharge) included in the costed programmes—see Appendix A, Table A.5
Kent North Downs and Medway	Chalk at outcrop	W	Artificial recharge of aquifer storage from the Medway to increase yield from the combined river and aquifer system	270	15	
South Lancs and North Cheshire Manchester/Warrington/ Altrincham area	Concealed Permo-Triassic sandstones	W	Artificial recharge of aquifer storage from the Dee to augment the combined aquifer/ surface storage/river system	230	30	
Glamorgan Cilfynidd, Taff valley	Terrace gravels	B	Recharge of final effluent from modern sewage works through gravels to produce raw water for potable supplies	45	2	
Sussex Hardham, near Pulborough	Syncline in Lower Greensand	B	Artificial recharge of aquifer storage, using Rother water, to provide maximum yield from combined system	90	5	

Appendix J The demand for water by industry

Introduction

J.1   This Appendix is concerned mainly with the use made of rivers by industry directly. The pattern of water use along rivers in industrial areas can be very complicated and the scope for generalisation is limited. The resources of these rivers can be extended by increased storage or import of water and by improved treatment of effluents. Any attempt to predict the need for these must take into account the scope for increased re-use—for instance, by suitable siting of factories and power stations in relation to sewage outfalls, as well as by greater internal recycling. Projections must of course also be made of future industrial activity and of changes in technology. The exercise will be unique to each river basin and will depend upon detailed studies, in co-operation with industrial users, by the water authority managing the basin. At the present, technological projections of water use, even over the fairly short term, are wholly lacking for many industries; and even in such fields as power generation 30-year projections of need are little more than speculation.

J.2   Nevertheless some attempt at generalisation has had to be made in order to hazard preliminary estimates of the probable impact, over the next generation, of industrial needs on the extent and pattern of water resource developments, especially on the need for storage and for bulk transmission. It is the purpose of this Appendix to outline some of the main features of industrial water use and to explain the options (e.g. between once through cooling and re-circulatory cooling); to provide a measure of justification for the assessments made in our regional studies, which call for very modest resource development on behalf of industrial abstractors; and to indicate from such figures as are available the general proportions of an industrial water balance diagram for England and Wales, bearing in mind that for the reasons given above this can be no more than a very tentative aid to an understanding of the situations in individual river basins.

Public and Private Supplies

J.3   Before public supplies of water were commonly available from public water undertakings a manufacturer who required supplies for his factory had to obtain them directly, either from boreholes or by siting his factory beside a river or a canal from which he could draw a supply and to which he would normally return his effluent. For those who use water in very large quantities, and whose quality requirements are not exacting, this is still the most common and the cheapest way of securing a supply. But for manufacturers who use smaller amounts and for whom a site on an aquifer or by a river is not conveniently available public water undertakings now provide a piped supply in most parts of the country; this accounts for about 15 per cent of all fresh water supplies to industry.

J.4   The Water Resources Act 1963 made it obligatory to get a licence and to pay a charge for a private supply. But it also made such a supply, once licensed, more secure. For users who have direct access to sources of adequate quality it is clearly more economic to increase these supplies than to take a supply of treated water by pipeline, so long as the required amount is available for abstraction. Even if the flow in a river may no longer be diminished by abstraction, the amount available may increase automatically as new sewage effluents are added upstream to the river flow, or it may be increased by regulating the river or importing water to increase its dry weather flow. When the latter becomes necessary, however, the cost is likely to increase substantially over that of a traditional riverside supply.

J.5   For economical water management every effort should be made to make direct supplies available for suitably sited industrial plant before resort is made to piped supplies. In some cases it may be possible to locate new industrial abstractors where supplies are more readily available (e.g. downstream rather than upstream of sewage effluent discharges) or to convey low-grade supplies to them via an industrial supply network. In other cases, where a high degree of reliability is not essential, it may be possible to guarantee supplies in most years by releasing water from public storage reservoirs more frequently.

Quantity and Quality Management

J.6   Since rivers both receive effluents and provide supplies, and since degradation of quality may inhibit certain uses, the maintenance of quality must be considered integrally with the flow balance. Effluents which help to maintain the quantity balance may intensify quality problems; treatment of effluents may be an alternative to dilution from regulating storage. In this respect the removal of pollutants by treatment plant, provided they can be recycled into the process or otherwise disposed of, is analogous with the dissipation of heat by cooling towers.

J.7   The maximum effective use of "direct" water supplies, within acceptable limits of flow and quantity, is the foundation of an acceptable and economic pattern of water use in industrial areas. The strategies proposed in this report are based on the assumption that every effort will be made to achieve this and, indeed, that most of the growth in industrial water needs will be met by increases in direct use, together with economies in water use within industry particularly by increased recycling.

Industrial Use of Water

J.8   During 1971 a daily average of nearly 5 million cubic metres of water was taken into industrial and commercial premises through metered connections from public water supply networks. A further 28 million cu.m.d. of fresh water were taken directly from rivers, canals and underground sources, mainly into power stations and into large manufacturing units, such as chemical plants, oil refineries, steelworks, paper and board mills and textile factories. Of this latter amount about 6 per cent came from boreholes and the remainder from surface sources.

J.9   The water obtained from the public supply is used mainly for personal services and for other purposes—such as food and drink processing—for which a "wholesome" as well as a fairly pure water is considered desirable. By and large this water is used only once in its potable state, after which much of it is discharged to public sewers; a pattern of use similar to that of water supplied for domestic purposes.

J.10   Of the water taken directly, especially from surface sources, much the most important single use is for cooling: for condensing steam at power stations (so that the condensate can be returned to the boilers for re-use) and carrying away the reject heat; for taking heat away from exothermic chemical processes so as to maintain the requisite reaction temperature; and for quenching hot products and hot wastes. But water also has an important role in transporting production materials and reagents into and around manufacturing sites and carrying away wastes. Sometimes the same water serves successive purposes on the same site; this may be described as *internal re-use*. More commonly water is *recycled* many times through the same plant, being stripped of its burden of heat (in a cooling tower) or waste (in a treatment plant) between each use.

J.11   A small fraction of the water abstracted directly is evaporated or otherwise used up in processes—e.g. by incorporation in a liquid product. Some is discharged into public sewers and thence to water-courses some distance away, as is most of that obtained from the public supply. But much the greater part is disposed of directly to the river from which it is drawn. Thereafter it is often abstracted again by another riparian user downstream; this may be described as *external re-use*.

J.12   Were it not for recycling, internal and external re-use[1] and the use of saline water for cooling, industry's total fresh water requirement would be about 140 million cu.m.d; ten times the total of public supplies. Together these factors reduce the net need to a fraction of total use, partly by reducing the total abstractive demand for fresh water (recycling; internal re-use; use of saline water) and partly by adding to the amounts available for abstraction, (external re-use).

Estimating Future Growth

J.13   Whereas therefore growth in demands on the public water supply can be related to prospective increases in use, since the water (in its potable state) is normally used only once, any prediction of the amounts needed to maintain direct supplies must take into account possible changes in patterns of re-use and recycling, and the substitution of saline waters.

J.14   In estimating future domestic needs account has been taken of estimates of future population, and allowance has been made for a growing per capita use as water using appliances become more widespread and new ones are introduced. Total domestic use is expected to double by 2001 or at some date in the following decade. And it has been assumed that piped supplies to industry, which equal about half of domestic use, will grow at the same rates. In assessing what new resources will be needed to meet the growth in public water supply, allowance has been made for specific cases where a second use for public supplies of water discharged as effluent is likely to be acceptable (as on the Thames) or may become possible in the future (as on the Trent).

J.15   It is not possible to make a useful assessment of the resources needed to maintain direct supplies by a similar method; that is to say, by predicting future use for each of the purposes for which water will be needed within factories and then adjusting the total to allow for re-use and substitution. It may never be possible to do this save in restricted areas of use (e.g. thermal power generation). Unless and until this can be done, one must proceed in some way from "proxy" indices (e.g. records of amounts abstracted under licence) which are related in a more or less arbitrary way to the total of industrial uses, on the one hand, and, on the other, to the net pressure these uses exert on resources.

J.16   Information about the extent of industrial abstractions has become available for the country as a whole only during the past three years, as a result of the Water Resources Act 1963. Application of an annual growth factor to the gross abstracted quantity, although it has been attempted, can really have little meaning, since it ignores changes in the other circumstances (substitution, re-use etc.) referred to above, which will affect net needs in each river basin. The relationship of net abstractive need to total industrial use is, indeed, largely the outcome of historical accident, since it depends upon the sequences in which plants are located along an industrial river, or even within an old-established factory complex. The period of record has been too short, in any case, to indicate any meaningful trend in abstracted quantity, and changes have been obscured by the errors and uncertainties of definition which inevitably afflict the first attempts to collate data in such a complex field.

J.17   In our regional studies, the total of recorded abstractions in each major river system was therefore adjusted, in the first instance, by a rather arbitrary net use factor, which was meant to reflect the apparent opportunities for successive re-abstraction of effluents returned by industrial users within that system. The term "net use", as employed here, means the effective depletion of flow in the river,

or at some particular point on the river course, as a result of a succession of abstractions and returns. Conversely it is the extra input needed to cope with a growing scale of abstraction and return without depletion of flow.

J.18   The effect of applying some annual growth rate to this net use was then considered. When the resulting net need was compared with the predicted growth in public water supplies and hence in sewage works effluents within each river basin it was concluded that in most areas the latter would more than suffice to meet any likely net growth in direct abstraction, provided that the abstraction points could be suitably located in relation to sewage outfalls. Only in a few industrial areas where such effluents could not be expected to make a contribution in the right place was allowance made for extra storage to meet increases in direct abstraction, or to meet a transfer of such demands to the public supply. It must be emphasised that such economy in water use will depend upon the future relative locations of sewage works and industrial abstractors, and that co-operation between water management authorities, local planning authorities and industrial users will be needed in order to achieve this.

J.19   The outcome of applying this rough and ready approach to the whole of England and Wales is that of the estimated new storage needed during the remaining years of this century, 80 per cent is designed to feed public water supply systems in the first instance, although much of this will find a second use (or, perhaps, many subsequent uses) on industrial premises and in a few instances water released from storage into regulated rivers may be used—say, as cooling water—before its abstraction into a public supply system. Only the remaining 20 per cent of new storage is envisaged specifically to meet net direct abstraction by industry.

J.20   It is true that hitherto little storage has been provided, outside the public supply system, to meet a direct industrial need and it may be asked why any other assumption requires justification. But, by and large, any further net abstractions of water in England and Wales will have to be balanced at times of low flow by releases from storage, and it may well prove that the allowances made in our studies for storage specifically to meet direct industrial demands will prove to have somewhat underestimated the real need.

Cooling Water Use by the Central Electricity Generating Board

J.21   In the case of the Central Electricity Generating Board, a rather less speculative approach has been possible. The CEGB is the largest single industrial user of water. In 1971 its abstraction of licensed fresh water was 18·9 million cu.m.d. (including 2·2 million cu.m.d. hydro power) plus a further abstraction of brackish water and seawater of 47 million cu.m.d. If these enormous needs are to be met, the CEGB must plan the general distribution of its stations and the incidence of its cooling water needs (96 per cent of all its requirements) for many years ahead. Moreover, the use of water in power stations is very much simpler to analyse than its uses in, say, certain areas of chemical manufacture. The CEGB has been able to tell us the proportion of its cooling load which is expected to fall on freshwater resources, and to confirm that future freshwater cooled stations will almost invariably employ recirculatory cooling and be sited where sewage effluents can contribute to their make-up needs.

J.22   The salient facts about current water use for power generation are readily available from the publications of the CEGB. As it happens the water needs of power generation on any definition (total use; total of abstractions; and consumption by evaporation) are very much greater than the corresponding needs of the whole of general industry and the greater certainty about the former therefore greatly facilitates the work of demand projection.

J.23   In any power station there is a vast quantity of heat to be dissipated to the environment. This can be transferred to surface waters by direct cooling circuits using either sea or river water. Alternatively, the heat may be dissipated to the atmosphere by passing the warmed water through cooling towers where the heat is transferred to the air mainly through the latent heat of evaporation. Roughly 1 per cent of the water throughput is evaporated in the process. Diagram J/1 shows, in diagrammatic form, alternative ways by which a typical heat load might be released to the environment. In each case 1 million cu.m.d leaves

---

1 These terms have been used rather differently in other publications. Recycling and internal re-use are sometimes grouped under a common title since they are both forms of economy practised by a single abstractor and their effects on the total of water abstracted may be indistinguishable. But whereas recycling, as defined here, is a means of effecting economy of water input to a single process, with predictable consequences and costs, internal re-use may be a side effect of a decision to associate new or altered processes on a given site or even to relocate such processes within the site. There is no *general* way of describing such opportunities or predicting the relevant costs, and the accidental nature of these opportunities has much in common with the accidents of external re-use by independent abstractors.

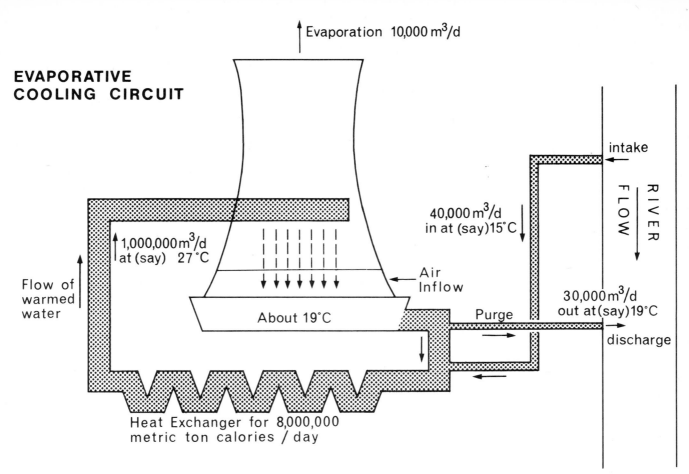

EVAPORATIVE COOLING CIRCUIT

Evaporation 10,000 m³/d

intake

RIVER FLOW

1,000,000 m³/d at (say) 27°C

40,000 m³/d in at (say) 15°C

Air Inflow

About 19°C

Flow of warmed water

Purge

30,000 m³/d out at (say) 19°C

discharge

Heat Exchanger for 8,000,000 metric ton calories / day

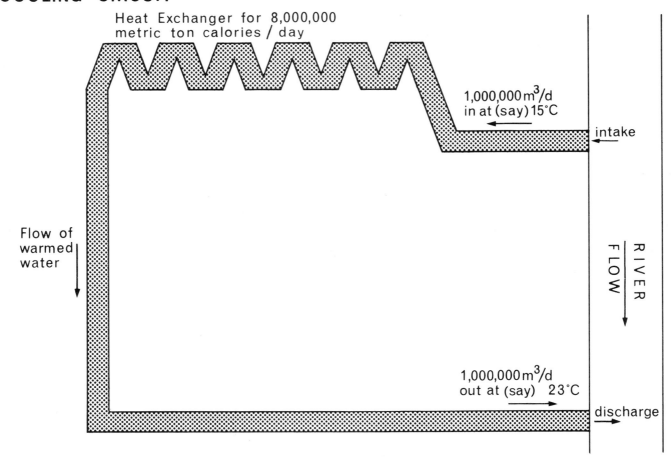

ONCE – THROUGH COOLING CIRCUIT

Heat Exchanger for 8,000,000 metric ton calories / day

1,000,000 m³/d in at (say) 15°C

intake

Flow of warmed water

RIVER FLOW

1,000,000 m³/d out at (say) 23°C

discharge

ALTERNATIVE COOLING ARRANGEMENTS

the condensers 8°C above its entry temperature; but whereas in the case of a once-through cooling circuit this heat is added to the river, in the case of evaporative cooling it is released to the atmosphere.

J.24 The total CEGB cooling load—that is to say the heat to be disposed of—depends upon the total power output, the selection of stations being operated at any time and the efficiency of each station. It can vary from about 140 per cent of the average on a mid-winter day to about 90 per cent of the average on a typical summer day. It is the summer load which is more critical for water resources.

J.25 The cooling load can conveniently be measured in metric ton calories (MTC).[1] In 1971 the average daily load was about 950 million MTC/day, requiring the use of about 105 million cu.m.d. of cooling water. The CEGB estimate that their electricity output might be trebled by the year 2001 and that the cooling throughput will be doubled. They expect the extra cooling load inland to be absorbed by cooling towers.

J.26 Table J.1 summarises the CEGB's use of water for cooling in 1971 with an indication of the possible use in 2001.

Table J.1
CEGB Use of Water for Cooling
million cu.m.d.

	1971	2001
Once-through cooling		
Seawater	47	100
Freshwater	18	—
Recirculation through cooling towers	40	100
Total throughput	105	200
Evaporation loss	0·4	1·5

J.27 Some 95 per cent of the CEGB's freshwater cooling load in 1971 was carried by four of the principal industrial river systems (Trent; Yorkshire; Mersey; Severn) and 55 per cent by the Trent alone. The cooling flow through power stations on the Trent is equivalent to 30 or 40 times the natural flow of that river under extreme conditions of dry weather.

Water Use by General Industry
J.28 Table J.2 below gives information about the average daily quantities of water directly abstracted by industry in 1971, derived from the returns by river authorities summarised in Appendix B of our Ninth Annual Report:

Table J.2
Water Use by Industry in 1971
million cu.m.d.

		General Industry	CEGB (for comparison)
(i)	Water consumed (mainly evaporated)	·29	·38
(ii)	Water returned but not locally[1] (to sewers, to sea or to neighbouring catchment)	·94	·17
(iii)	Water returned locally with impaired quality	·89	·78
(iv)	Water returned locally without significant deterioration in quality	7·00	17·50
		9·12	18·83

Note: 1 Given by difference

Cooling Load of General Industry
J.29 There is evidence to suggest that some 2 million cu.m.d. of the water in category (iv) is used for generating water power and for gravel and coal washing; the rest is mainly cooling water. Some of the water in category (iii) would be used, as well as for process purposes, to carry heat to waste; and most of the evaporative loss in category (i) can be attributed to recirculatory cooling systems. On the assumption that 5 million cu.m.d. in categories (iii) and (iv) served as coolant with a mean temperature rise of 9°C and that 250 thousand cu.m.d. in category (i) was evaporated in cooling circuits, the general industrial cooling load can be estimated as follows:

1 1 MTC is the amount of heat required to raise the temperature of 1 cubic metre of water by 1 °C.

$$5\,000\,000 \times \quad 9 = 45\,000\,000$$
$$250\,000 \times 830 = 207\,000\,000$$

Total (say) 250 000 000 MTC/day

This is about half the CEGB freshwater cooling load. The corresponding cooling water circulating might amount to between 25 million and 30 million cu.m.d. About half of the load is located on the four industrial river systems referred to in paragraph J.27.

The Heavy Industry Sector
J.30 Table J.3 provides information, obtained by enquiry of selected firms, about the demand for water in the steel industry and important sections of the chemical and petroleum industries, which between them account for some 20 per cent of the fresh water taken into premises in the manufacturing industry; and which together with the CEGB account for two-thirds of the fresh water taken into industrial premises. These industries are, like thermal power generation, mainly established along the lower courses of rivers, beside estuaries or on the coast. Together they account for much of the industrial cooling load and they usually have access either to river flows augmented by sewage effluents or to saline water to meet this large requirement.

Table J.3
Combined Water Demand by Heavy Industry
(Steel, Heavy Chemicals (part), Oil Refining (part))

	Average amounts million cu.m.d.
Freshwater:	
Supplies from public water undertakings	0·8
Abstractions from rivers and canals	1·5
Abstractions of groundwater	0·1
Seawater:	
Abstraction	5·6
Cooling water:	
Through cooling flow—fresh	1·0
—saline	5·6
Evaporative loss (fresh)	0·2[1]
Total cooling circulation	25·0

Note: 1 Apart from water evaporated in quenching products and wastes (0·1 to 0·2 million cu.m.d.)

The Total Cooling Load
J.31 The power and heavy industry sectors identified above account for some 1200 million MTC/day of cooling load (paragraphs J.25 and J.29). The total cooling load in England and Wales may well be of the order of 1300 million MTC/day represented by a cooling flow of some 135 million cu.m.d. Changes in this load are likely to be a function of fuel consumption and of growth in general industrial activity, and may possibly be related to future investment or employment figures.

J.32 Such growth may then be divided into prospective fresh and sea water needs and the former partly converted to equivalent evaporative requirements, involving both cooling tower construction and provision for evaporation loss and purge.

J.33 Only 15 per cent of water cooling in the selected heavy industries and power generation is at present carried by once-through streams of fresh water and the same percentage can probably be applied throughout industry. Any increase in the cooling load could therefore readily be taken up by using saline water (once-through) or cooling towers, and there is no reason to look for growth in the use of once-through freshwater cooling beyond that conveniently available from new effluent flows.

J.34 It is likely that heavy industry will continue to concentrate in coastal zones and along the lower reaches of rivers, leaving the bulk of other industries, which account for most of the industrial demand on the public water supply, to locate themselves further upstream or elsewhere inland. There is no reason to expect sudden changes in the rate of growth of industrial demands on the public water supply; there is, however, reason to expect that effluents generated by increases in public water supply will be available to meet the needs of the major industrial users abstracting river water downstream, and will be sufficient, when accompanied by changes in cooling practice, to accommodate most of those needs.

J.35 It has been estimated that public water supply needs will require the provision of some 12 million cu.m.d. of new primary resources (i.e. resources derived from storage rather than re-use) by 2001. If this amount were made available, after discharge as sewage effluent, for a single evaporative cooling circuit with a ratio of one part evaporation to three parts purge it would sustain a cooling capacity of some 3000 million MTC/day, some $3\frac{1}{2}$ times the present freshwater-based cooling capacity and 15 times the present through-cooling by fresh water. If almost wholly evaporated (because, for instance, the purge requirements of a series of power stations along one river would not be additive) it would sustain a cooling load much greater still.

Growth in Categories of Industrial Use

J.36 It is evident therefore that if evaporative cooling can be taken for granted at all future (freshwater) installations there is no prima facie need to consider providing additional primary sources for this purpose. On this basis the suggested provision for increased public water supplies should also cope, directly or indirectly by effluents, for the growth in demand for water consumed by evaporation (category (i) in Table J.2) and for water returned locally without significant deterioration in quality (category (iv)), including those CEGB requirements which fall in those categories, provided that abstraction and discharge points can be suitably located.

J.37 Water returned locally with impaired quality (category (iii)), which includes purge from evaporative cooling systems, cannot readily be distinguished, in terms of availability for re-use, from category (iv). It is probable that much of the water in category (iii) carries waste heat in addition to any other pollution-load. It may be discharged in close proximity to discharges in category (iv), and below the point of discharge they will combine in a common mixture with the remainder of the river flow.

J.38 But whereas a once-through cooling load (category (iv)) can be taken over by evaporative cooling it may not be equally convenient, or even possible, to cope with an expanding waste load by installing effluent treatment plant. Depending on the difficulty of treatment and the terms of future consents to discharge, increasing industrial activity could be accompanied by either an increase or a decrease in the volume of effluent in category (iii) at particular sites. However, on the assumption that additional storage will not normally be provided to dilute wastes carried in rivers, and bearing in mind the expected generation of some 12 million cu.m.d. of new sewage effluents, it does not seem necessary to contemplate any separate provision for growth in category (iii)—amounting at present to about $1\frac{1}{2}$ million cu.m.d. including the CEGB uses—apart from the provision already made for industrial areas not well placed to re-use future domestic effluents.

J.39 Much of the water returned remotely (category (ii)) must be water disposed of into public sewerage systems, and its availability for further use will depend upon the circumstances of its eventual return to the river system. It is estimated that about 60 per cent of it passes into sewerage systems which discharge their effluents directly to the sea or to estuaries, as does some 40 per cent of the public water supply, and an increase in either of these will be at the expense of flows in rivers. However, although the circumstances of disposal of water in category (ii) are exceptional, abstractions in this category can be met out of the general increase in effluent contribution to the river system (more than half of the 12 million cu.m.d. of new sewage effluents) just as readily as abstractions in the other three categories. There seems therefore to be no argument for making special provision to meet abstractions in this category, in the generality of industrial areas.

Extrapolation of Demand on River System

J.40 It is evident that there is no general formula for calculating the effective direct industrial demand on the river system in the area of a river authority or a regional water authority. There are localities where convenient access to sewage effluents will simply not be available unless arrangements are made for the recovery and distribution of effluents from tidal outfalls. There are other areas (the majority) where such effluents are likely to be adequate in volume and location, but it is impossible to prove that every would-be abstractor in these areas will be conveniently served at the abstraction point of his choice. It is

unlikely to be helpful to attempt to extrapolate future demand on river systems directly from any estimate of present demand.

J.41 As more data becomes available, a more fruitful approach will be to calculate the minimum flows needed to meet the existing pattern of use on any river system, including flows needed to by-pass factory sites and the flow needed to enter the estuary. It will then be possible to set up alternative flow (and quality) balances for possible future patterns of use on that river system allowing, inter alia, for changes in cooling practice. This involves simulation of the river system in a variety of possible patterns, which may be represented by residual flow diagrams, and will lead in due course to the integral design of the system.

General Water Balance Diagram

J.42 From information now available in the River Pollution Survey[1] and in the statistics of abstractions resulting from the licensing procedure under the Water Resources Act, 1963, it is possible to construct a rudimentary water balance diagram for England and Wales which indicates the relationships between many of the quantities referred to above. It should be emphasised that the actual balance will vary widely from one river basin to another. Diagram J/2 is an extreme simplification of a system in which numerous abstractions and returns of water will succeed one another in a pattern unique to each river, but it provides an understanding of the system and the ways in which it can develop.

J.43 The river flow represented in Diagram J/2 is a combined value, in extreme dry weather, for the rivers of England and Wales. In practice some water will drain directly through aquifers and coastal creeks to the sea. The other figures represent average daily quantities for 1971. The total dry weather flow to the sea is assumed to be composed, in these circumstances, of some 18 million cu.m.d. of natural drainage through the river channel and some 14 million cu.m.d. of public water supplies, assumed to come out of reservoir or aquifer storage (top of diagram). Industry also uses some groundwater sources of its own. The total of inputs is thus some 34 million cu.m.d.

J.44 The use of a composite diagram to represent all rivers naturally understates the impact on those rivers most heavily used by industry. On the other hand the representation of all abstraction at two points on the course of the river greatly exaggerates the depletion of flow in critical reaches.

J.45 A similar diagram (J/3) indicates a plausible balance for the year 2001. The estimates for supplies from storage resources (mainly public water supply) are those given elsewhere in this report. The figures which indicate a pattern of use in industry, on the other hand, cannot be assessed with any confidence for a date so far ahead. Nevertheless, the diagram indicates how industrial water use might be substantially increased without detriment to the quantitative balance of the river system (indeed, dry weather flows at some critical points in the system have been improved) provided that through cooling with river water is not unduly increased. In Diagram J/3 total cooling flows and process streams have been approximately doubled in scale without changing the amounts of fresh water used for through cooling. If current expectations of improved thermal efficiency and increased cooling water temperature range at power stations are borne out, this might correspond with a three-fold increase in power output.

J.46 It is clear that many alternative balance diagrams could be prepared on the basis of the indicated increase in storage resources; and that very much more industrial use could be provided for whilst improving dry weather flows in rivers. For instance, through cooling with river water could be diminished or eliminated (as envisaged in Table J.1), so enabling dry weather flows to be further increased in critical reaches. Improved economy in river water use for process purposes (represented by combined abstractions of about six million cu.m.d. in Diagram J/3) would have a similar effect.

J.47 Nevertheless, the achievement of such a balance must depend on the proper location of outfalls and abstraction points in planned relation to one another, and would be vitiated by a completely haphazard pattern of development.

1 River Pollution Survey of England and Wales: Updated 1972. Issued by the Department of the Environment and the Welsh Office. HMSO 1972

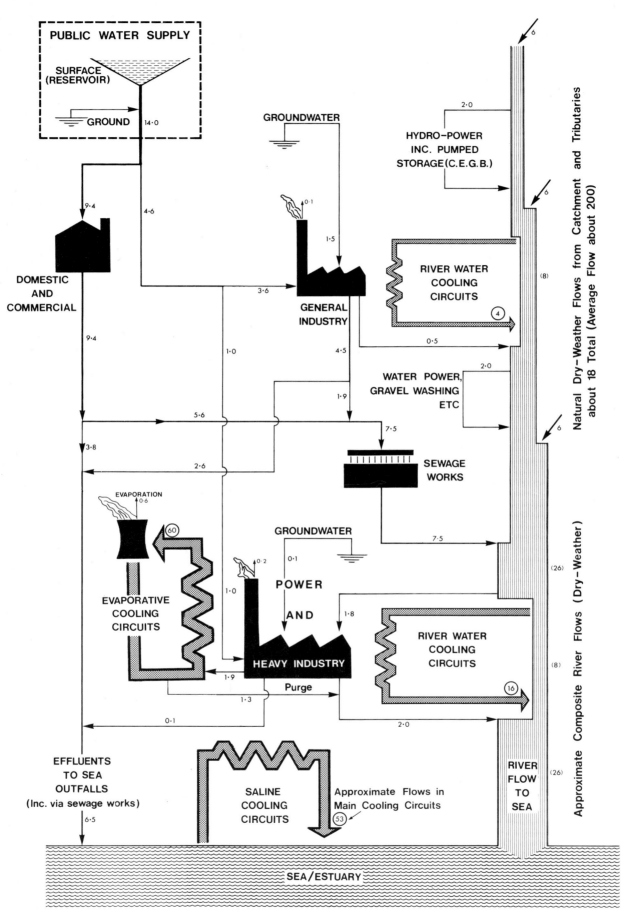

WATER BALANCE DIAGRAM FOR ENGLAND AND WALES : 1971

(Average Quantities in Million Cubic Metres / Day)

DIAGRAM J/2

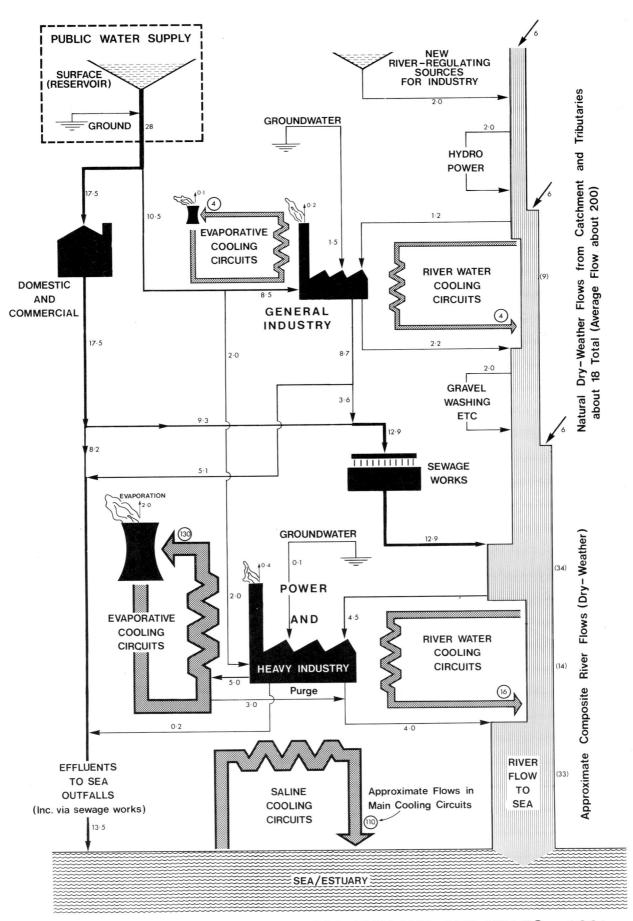

WATER BALANCE DIAGRAM FOR ENGLAND AND WALES : 2001
(Average Quantities in Million Cubic Metres/Day)

Summary of Arguments

J.48 It is suggested that although fresh water taken into industrial premises (including power plants) in England and Wales amounted in 1971 only to about 33 million cu.m.d. on average (85 per cent of it is taken directly from sources) the aggregate of freshwater uses in industry, including re-use, was equivalent to about 90 million cu.m.d. In addition some 53 million cu.m.d. of saline water were used.

J.49 The total cooling load was probably about 1300 million MTC per day, nearly three-quarters of it accounted for by the CEGB. Cooling probably accounted for about 95 per cent of the total of fresh and saline water uses (over 140 million cu.m.d.) within industry.

J.50 Although no general definition has been offered of the net use of water for all purposes in a river system which will lend itself to extrapolation and thus to prediction of future needs, one can examine possible future water balances, incorporating assumptions about future cooling practice, and consider the extent to which they will provide for expansion in the various categories of industrial water use.

J.51 This broad examination has been facilitated by the division of industry into two groups, one of which accounts for much the greater part of industrial use from public sources and the other ("heavy" industry plus power generation) for almost the whole of industrial use from private sources and for almost the whole of the industrial cooling load. The latter group is well placed to re-use future sewage effluents.

J.52 On the basis of an approximate doubling of storage-based resources for public water supply, leading to an increase of possibly 30 per cent in the gross dry weather flows of rivers, a plausible future balance diagram provides for a doubling of the industrial cooling load and of other water uses within industry, mainly by increasing the capacity of evaporative cooling circuits. Thus the increase of storage-based resources from some 14 million cu.m.d. to 28 million cu.m.d. (14 per cent of average run-off from England and Wales) could correspond with a growth in total industrial use from about 140 million cu.m.d. to over 280 million cu.m.d. (Diagram J/3).

J.53 It therefore makes sense to assume that a great expansion in industrial water use need not involve any commensurate expansion of primary (i.e. storage-based) resources, even on the assumption that direct abstractors cannot be permitted, save in a few exceptional cases, to make further inroads into natural dry weather flows.

J.54 Our planning has assumed the need to expand primary (i.e. storage-based) resources on the same scale as the expected growth in public water use, excepting for a few special cases where re-use should add to the resources available for public supply; but primary resources for direct industrial use have been added to these only on a very limited scale, in a few areas where it has been thought prudent to make special provision.

J.55 These assumptions imply the siting of large scale water users at points in the river system where their needs can be met (or, in appropriate cases, in places where they can use seawater for cooling) as well as a great extension of evaporative cooling installations.

J.56 More generally they call for the continuous "design" by river basin management authorities of the pattern of abstractions, uses and discharges along industrial river systems so as to maintain a viable and efficient water balance in terms of both quantity and quality; and the organisation and means to put these plans into effect.

Appendix K Diagrams of source development programmes

This Appendix comprises a series of 20 diagrams to illustrate a selection of programmes covering the range of strategies described in Chapter 8 and summarised in Table 16.

The diagrams are:

2 Diagrams 1/1 and 1/2: Strategic Source-Demand System at 1981

Show the sources to be developed and aqueduct links for transmitting water to the deficiency centres required by 1981.

1/1	:	Recommended Development All strategies except F
1/2	:	Full Regional Self-Sufficiency— Strategy F

8 Diagrams 2/A1–2/G2 : Strategic Source-Demand System at 2001

These show the sources to be developed and aqueduct links for transmitting the water to the deficiency centres required by 2001.

2/A1	:	Programme A1 All Inland Storage—Least Cost Solution
2/B1	:	Programme B1 Maximum Use of Estuary Storage
2/C1	:	Programme C1 Limited Number of Large Reservoirs and Dee Estuary Storage No new surface storage in South East
2/C2	:	Programme C2 Limited Number of Large Reservoirs and Dee Estuary Storage One inland reservoir in South East
2/C4	:	Programme C4 Limited Number of Large Reservoirs, Dee and Wash Estuary Storage No new inland reservoir in South East
2/D3	:	Programme D3 Limited Number of Large Reservoirs,

Dee Estuary Storage, Trent Quality Improvement and London Basin Recharge

2/F1	:	Programme F1 Full Regional Self-sufficiency All Inland Storage
2/G2	:	Programme G2 Partial Regional Self-sufficiency Inland Storage, Wash Estuary Storage, London Basin Recharge

8 Diagrams 3/A1–3/G2 : Future Source Development

These show the dates at which the sources are required to be introduced to meet the estimated growth of demand.

Individual titles as for 2/A1–2/G2 respectively.

1 Diagram 4/C2 : Assumed Flow Pattern in Strategic Source-Demand System 1981–2001 Programme C2 (One Variation of Preferred Strategy)

This diagram shows for one programme within the preferred strategy of mixed inland and estuary storage, the assumed flow pattern in key links and quantities to be supplied from associated sources in the period 1981–2001.

1 Diagram 5/C2 : Total and Discounted Annual Expenditure (Capital and Running Costs) Programme C2 (One Variation of Preferred Strategy)

This diagram shows for the same programme the year by year incidence of expenditure required to implement the programme, including running costs. The diagram also shows these annual costs discounted to 1974 at the recommended Treasury discount rate of 10 per cent.

1   Water Supplies in South East England 1966 (out of print)
2   Morecambe Bay Barrage: Desk Study: Report of Consultants. HMSO 1966 £1.12½ (£1.24)
3   Solway Barrage: Desk Study: Report of Consultants. HMSO 1966 80p (89½p)
4   Morecambe and Solway Barrages: Report on Desk Studies 1966 (out of print)
5   Interim Report on Water Resources in the North. HMSO 1967 60p (66½p)
6   Report on Desalination for England and Wales. HMSO 1969 20p (22½p)
7   Water Resources in the North: Northern Technical Working Party Report. HMSO 1970 £9.50 (£9.87)
8   Water Resources in the North: Report by the Water Resources Board. HMSO 1970 £1.80 (£1.86)
9   The Groundwater Hydrology of the Lincolnshire Limestone 1969 £7.00
10 The Wash: Estuary Storage: Report of the Desk Study. HMSO 1970 £1.05 (£1.14)
11 Water Resources in Wales and the Midlands: Report by the Water Resources Board. HMSO 1971 £1.50 (£1.59)
12 Morecambe Bay: Estuary Storage: Report by the Water Resources Board. HMSO 1972 90p (97½p)
13 Morecambe Bay: Estuary Storage: Report by the Economic Study Group. HMSO 1972 £1.90 (£2.11)
14 Artificial Recharge of the London Basin I—Hydrogeology 1972 £4.00
15 The Generation of Synthetic River Flow Data 1972 £3.35
16 Modelling of Groundwater and Surface Water Systems I—Theoretical Relationships between Groundwater Abstraction and Base Flow 1972 £1.60
17 Desalination 1972. HMSO 1972 36½p (40p)
18 The Trent Research Programme Volume I: Report by the Water Resources Board. HMSO 1973 60p (65½p)
19 Artifical Recharge of the London Basin II—Electrical Analogue Model Studies (in press)
20 Groundwater Resources of the Vale of Clwyd (in press)
21 A Simulation Model of the Upstream Movement of Anadromous Salmonid Fish (in press)
22 Water Resources in England and Wales Volume I: Report (in press)
The Surface Water Year Book of Great Britain Supplement 1965. HMSO £1.37½ (£1.51)
The Surface Water Year Book of Great Britain 1965–66. HMSO £4.00 (£4.25)
The Groundwater Year Book 1964–66. HMSO £10.00 (£10.21)
The Groundwater Year Book 1967. HMSO £10.00 (£10.21)
The Hydrogeology of the London Basin (£10.15)

Publications Nos 9, 14, 15, 16 (and 19, 20 and 21 when printed) and The Hydrogeology of the London Basin are obtainable only from the Water Resources Board, Reading Bridge House, Reading RG1 8PS

Prices in brackets include postage.

Printed in London for Her Majesty's Stationery Office by McCorquodale Printers Ltd.
Dd. 505928   K16